THE FIRST FIVE MINUTES

Other Books by Norman King

The Money Messiahs

Big Sales from Small Spaces

Dan Rather

How to Turn Your Home into a Money Factory

The Prince and the Princess: A Love Story

Here's Erma: The Bombecking of America

The Money Market Book

All in the First Family (co-written with Bill Adler)

The First Five Minutes

The Successful Opening Moves in Business, Sales & Interviews

NORMAN KING

PRENTICE HALL PRESS

New York London Toronto Sydney Tokyo

Published by Prentice Hall Press
A Division of Simon & Schuster, Inc.
Gulf+Western Building
One Gulf+Western Plaza
New York, NY 10023

PRENTICE HALL PRESS is a trademark of Simon & Schuster, Inc.

Library of Congress Cataloging-in-Publication Data

King, Norman, 1926–
  The first five minutes.
  1. Conduct of life. 2. Business etiquette.
3. Success. I. Title. II. Title: First 5 minutes.
BJ1595.K46   1987   650.1   86-25232
ISBN 0-13-318404-8

Designed by C. Linda Dingler
Manufactured in the United States of America
10 9 8 7 6 5

To William B. Williams—
*a friend for all seasons
and for all reasons*

CONTENTS

INTRODUCTION:
A POSITIVE IMAGE FOR
SUCCESS

To the average onlooker, success in any chosen endeavor is usually seen as a kind of magical fluke, a "lucky" turn, a sudden breakthrough to triumph.

Nothing could be further from the truth.

The fact is that there is no such thing as magic, luck, *or* "instant" success these days. Success of any kind must be prepared for constantly in a practical and everyday manner so that when the propitious moment arrives you can take advantage of it—and win!

That is the reason the first five minutes of any interrelationship is of such extreme and crucial importance, and why it is the subject of this book. Those three hundred seconds are the true culmination of years of hard work, patient study, and constant attempts at self-improvement, adjustments made so that you will be able to project the *real* you.

That is the reason you need to spend a lifetime of preparation in order to make that five-minute introduction to another person count the most. Only then can you use those five minutes to successfully impress your own positive image on someone else in true communication that *means something*.

If properly prepared, such a positive image can project a powerful charisma in those crucial minutes that will make an indelible and everlasting impression.

You must take serious steps, however, to prepare this "image for success" that becomes the key to your effectiveness in using those first five minutes. Your positive image for success is made up of a number of important factors: integrity, confidence, presence, certainty, understanding, credibility, authority, vivacity, and even-temperedness, not necessarily in that order.

Each facet of your personality is a block in the façade you are building in the edifice of your success.

To put you in control of these key factors of personality and character—and the way you project them in your persona—you must first of all have an attitude of confidence, of businesslike resolve, and of integrity.

You demonstrate this in the way you carry yourself, in the way you dress, in the way you speak, and in what you say when you do speak.

Charisma and "style" will flow from you only if you have the right opinion of yourself, if you are not playing some game that you do not believe in, if you honestly let show feelings that are intrinsically real.

This book is planned to take you step by step through a number of important points in character projection. It will provide you with exercises to control your breathing when you are speaking, will give you tips even on such obvious matters as dressing for a projection of authority, and so on.

You will be able to go through check lists to test yourself on personality aspects as well as on physical points of grooming. You will find hints on how to assemble yourself into an integrated whole.

By the time you have thoroughly gained control over your mind, your body, and your environment—with this book as a guide—*then* you will be ready to use that five minutes for every important encounter.

In addition to preparing you to deliver that positive image for success at every appearance, this book will enable you to learn specific rules for mounting a perfect job interview, for making a crucial sales pitch, for impressing people instantly on the office scene, and even for establishing and maintaining total and unassailable self-assurance.

If you study this book seriously and take advantage of its many tips and pieces of advice from the famous as well as the not-so-famous but successful, you will be able to grasp that "instant success" you have seen so many others achieve.

Good luck!

THE FIRST FIVE MINUTES

1

THE IMPORTANCE
OF SCORING QUICKLY

Five minutes is all it takes.

The first five minutes when you meet a stranger for a business meeting is a crucial time for both of you.

By the time the second hand has traveled five times around your wristwatch, two things will have happened:

You will have decided exactly how much you trust or distrust your business acquaintance

and

the other person will have decided exactly how much he or she trusts or distrusts you.

The marketplace is crowded with instances of meeting people; everybody's business life is. But in each meeting the most important part of that relationship is established magically and ineluctably within that vital first five minutes.

WORD FROM THE MOUNTAINTOP

Lee Iacocca, the man with the one-two punch who was Father of the Mustang at Ford and the Resurrector at Chrysler, put it in focus in his best-selling autobiography:

I learned [how] to figure people out pretty quickly. To this day, I can usually tell a fair amount about somebody from our first meeting.

Here is a man with a proven track record in business who makes no bones about it: Those first five minutes are as important for him as for the person he is sizing up.

Put yourself in the place of the man facing a giant like Iacocca. You can see that those five minutes must be handled with total precision. They are five minutes that you can never retrieve for another try. You live or you die by them.

PUTTING THAT BEST FOOT FORWARD

It is, therefore, of signal importance for you to establish yourself by what is called "putting your best foot forward" in that crucial three hundred seconds. Those moments can never be materially changed without a great deal of hard labor and under almost insurmountable odds, reminiscent of the labors of Sisyphus, who was sentenced by the gods to roll a huge boulder up a steep incline for eternity.

Let me give you an example of a meeting and how those first five minutes evolved.

Recently I had a business lunch with a Fortune 500 chief executive officer about an important business deal. I had never before met him. I knew that as soon as I sat down at our luncheon meeting, the initial impression I made would be the impression that would determine whether we proceeded together or not.

Everything went wrong. I was late to the meeting but tried to pass it off as easily as I could. Yet I was not with him for more than five minutes when he turned to me and said:

"I like you. I think I would like to do business with you."

CONVERSING IN SMALL TALK

Later on, when I looked back on what we had talked about during that five-minute period, I realized quite clearly that it could not be what we had said to each other that put me into his good graces, and him in mine. We had been speaking in what would be termed small talk; a bit of sociological chatter, something to do with current news events, an item here and there about politics, about which I always keep *au courant*, and, of course, about business.

But I could not recall anything *serious*—you know, any big-deal earth-shattering thoughts.

It was the *way* our personas stepped forward to meet each other that made that meeting a success. It was the *manner* in which we perceived each other, the way we each put out signals to the other, by which we established a communicative bridgehead to each other.

In fact, as I discussed my business meeting with a friend, I was immediately asked:

"Hey, what did you *say* to him? You must really have impressed him!"

Yet I had to admit that I could not put my finger on any specific detail. And I realized a strange fallacy widespread among people. Most people think it is *what* you say that is important and not *how* you say it.

LUNCHEON FOR TWO

A latecomer rushes up to a diner seated at a table in a restaurant.

"I'm sorry I'm late," the latecomer says.
"That's perfectly all right," the diner says.

Seems a fairly cut-and-dried exchange.
But is it?
For a moment I would like to examine that exchange from the standpoint of delivery—*how* the people speak their lines rather than *what* they say.

First Take

"I'm sorry I'm late," delivered in a breathless haste, with an apologetic nod, is a simple and open-handed excuse. It is an apology that has been offered in the hopes that it will be accepted.

"That's perfectly all right," delivered in a smiling way, means that the excuse *is* accepted at face value.

But there might be a different kind of exchange, using exactly the same words.

Second Take

"I'm sorry I'm late," uttered with stiff-lipped disdain, means exactly the opposite of apology. It means that the latecomer has deliberately delayed his entrance in order to impress, in one way or another, the diner.

"That's perfectly all right," snapped out with an equal amount of enraged insolence, means that the apology is *not* accepted and that the tardiness is *not* "all right."

And there might even be a third type of communication.

Third Take

"I'm sorry I'm late," spoken in a low-keyed, intense tone of respectful apology, means the latecomer knows he has offended someone who obviously is a superior. He is hoping for a reprieve.

"That's perfectly all right," said in an icy, distant, and aloof tone of dismissal means the diner is absolutely fed up in advance with the subordinate who is trying to impress him.

And there is a fourth type of exchange.

Fourth Take

"I'm sorry I'm late," uttered in a casual, throwaway manner, means the latecomer cares little about the person with whom he or she is dining. To the latecomer, the diner is lucky he or she has arrived at all.

"That's perfectly all right," whispered in a hoarse-voiced, contrite manner, means the diner knows that something has occurred that has thrown the meeting into a holding pattern for the time being. Maybe later.

Note that in all of the preceding exchanges, the words—the verbal content—are exactly the same. It is the nonverbal content—the tone of voice, the set of the body, the facial expression, the eyes—that differs.

That is the first point you must remember about putting yourself over to someone else during that first business contact. Communication involves two different levels, both verbal and nonverbal. You must consider them both important, with nonverbal probably counting for more than verbal.

THE POLITE WAY TO MEET

In the case of my own meeting with the Fortune 500 CEO, I spoke exactly those words to him myself. I was trying to apologize for an egregious breach of common courtesy. You simply do *not* waltz in late to a luncheon engagement with someone you are trying to impress.

I uttered those words as graciously as I could in an effort to convince him of my sincerity, to offer my humble apologies for inconveniencing him, and to ask for his forgiveness even before we got down to ordering luncheon. He was one up on me already, and we had not even begun to pass the time of day before thinking about what we were going to eat.

He actually responded in the same vein, being gracious enough to realize I had been detained in some way that I could not control, and accepted my apologies and let me know he did not feel put upon by my lateness. He *knew* he was one up on me already, but he was not going to hold it against me. The way in which he expressed himself to me made it clear that he was willing to see how things were going to develop between us before making up his mind about me.

MANKIND'S CODE OF MANNERS

Every one of us is a human organism dedicated to surviving in a hostile and unfriendly world. Our responses to outward stimuli are usually of an aggressive nature. Only infrequently is the organism able to respond with affection and with total lack of fear. The thin veneer that makes man a social animal and provides him with a seeming air of gentility is his code of manners.

Like all living organisms, the human animal recognizes physical dangers and tries to steer clear of them: fire, ice, water, falls from heights, and so on. It is other human animals that can provide the most trouble, that is, in plain terms, "the other guy." The rules of society—those "manners" just mentioned—are there to keep the human animal in check and make interaction easier.

When two people meet today in a business situation, there is immediately an automatic and primeval probing, in spite of our veneer of civilized demeanor. The handshake has been popular for centuries. It proves that the individual with the open hand does not hold a knife or weapon in it with which to threaten the other person. The handshake is a symbolic gesture.

The truly evil individual may well clutch a sharp rock or other lethal weapon in the other, hidden, hand. Nevertheless, the handshake must be considered a symbol of friendship and trust, in spite of such subtleties.

CONVERSATION AND CONSIDERATION

There is a great deal more to human probing than simply the gesture of being unarmed. People use speech as well as movements in order to understand and enter into one another's mind-set and psyche. Understanding and entering into another's thought processes is accomplished by the civilized method of simple conversation, the thing that makes those first five minutes of a business meeting so extremely important.

Language has its roots in commerce. Among peoples who speak different languages, the initial contact may well be over business of some kind, buying and selling.

During any military action, the first thing soldiers in a strange land learn is to translate the give and take of commerce into some understandable *lingua franca*.

"How much for this?"
"How much you pay, Joe?"

And so on.

Whenever you open your mouth to speak, you are going to disclose something about yourself. The way you phrase a question, the way you unburden yourself of an opinion, and the general stylistic and nonverbal manner in which you speak reveals almost everything there is to know about you.

When you talk, the listener hears what you have to say and makes inferences not only on the basis of the logic and sense of what you say but on the basis of *how* you say it. Even so, no one should base total judgment and evaluation on only that first impression. Most people know how erroneous a first impression can be, especially when it is based on such slim evidence. Most people hold off a little in order to gather more information before fashioning a response.

PICKING UP CONVERSATIONAL CLUES

There is, nevertheless, a strong tendency to judge and evaluate others with great certainty during the first moments of communication. For example:

- The person who speaks softly is judged to be shy.
- The person who speaks loudly is judged to be aggressive or bold.
- The person who speaks in a moderate tone is judged to be neither too shy nor too bold.

Note that establishing a business rapport between two people is very much like constructing a house with little building blocks. As each piece of information becomes available through dialogue, you begin to build up a structure. If you place one building block out of line at an angle to the wall, it affects the way you lay all the other blocks after it.

Suppose the person with whom you are talking comes across as too strong in one way or another, or comes across as too weak. Your reaction to either of these impressions may cause you to place one of these building blocks out of line. Anything that the other person does that is exaggerated in any way or that appears to be out of the ordinary tends to lead you to place a building block a skewed angle.

THE FIRST IMPRESSION LASTS

We can go one step further than Lee Iacocca. The first impression is all-important; it tends usually to be irreversible. Any extreme type of behavior thus sets up a bias for all your subsequent perceptions of the person to whom you are talking. You can revise your initial impression later on, but first perceptions tend to be most lasting and are difficult to shake up and change.

The point I am making here should be obvious, but it may not be obvious to someone who does not understand his or her own out-of-sync manners. A nervous tic, a tendency to stutter, a frantic clutch for a cigarette—every one of these starts you off negatively in an encounter.

Centuries of accumulated wisdom and societal regimen have established a traditional *modus operandi* of social intercourse. If you deviate at all from this rather rigid but elegantly conceived method of interaction, you will find yourself observed *in extremis* and quite probably placed outside the pale of ordinary conventional behavior by the person observing you.

At the same time, conventional behavior changes from day to day, sometimes with great rapidity. Males with long hair were not tolerated until the 1970s. Nor were beards and mustaches considered conventional grooming. Now they are acceptable. Four-letter words were never used in polite society until the late 1960s. You must proceed carefully with them even today; not all levels of society tolerate such words. For every one that does not, another does, and reveres them. Try to figure that out.

WHAT GOES? WHAT DOESN'T?

How do you know what to say in order to impress someone else?

Unfortunately, there is no simple or fixed rule. In certain levels of society, you can impress by the particular type of job you hold, by your status in the business world. However, in another layer of society, such status means nothing and simply points up your lack of importance. In fact, in some social circles, "job" or "profession" means nothing. Social skills, the ability to tell a good story, the skill of emanating "style" and "charisma," the genius of being warm and friendly, these mean more to people not interested in job status or the possession of money to the exclusion of all else.

I do believe there is one rule that you can follow, no matter where you are, and no matter whom you are trying to impress. Try to communicate honestly about who you are rather than trying to paint a favorable, but untrue, picture of yourself. If you portray yourself inaccurately in public, you are sure to be caught and forced to correct the picture, especially if there are future meetings. Why force yourself into a position that could prove embarrassing for you tomorrow simply to make a point today that will mean nothing in the long run?

THE CHAMELEONS AMONG US

This point about honesty brings up a rather interesting study in human psychology. There are basically two types of people, or perhaps I should say two types of *behavior* in people. There are those people who want to fit in at all costs, and there are those who care little about fitting in.

The easiest way to "belong" to a group is to assume the protective coloration of people in it. For that reason, psychologists call people who *do* want to fit in "social chameleons," because they usually assume the attitudes and outer manifestations of those they want to emulate.

On the other end of the scale, of course, are the rugged individualists who make no point of trying to fit in but who are always themselves to a degree that is infuriating to people with an understanding of sociology. These are people I would call "leopards" (after the Biblical question in Isaiah: "Can the leopard [change] his spots?").

Tests show that there is some chameleon and some leopard in all of us, but in some the chameleon element dominates and in others the leopard element does. Each one of us is actually somewhere at a point between these two extremes.

To explore the concept further, the chameleon is an adept reader of other people. In the words of Mark Snyder, a social psychologist at the University of Minnesota, these chameleons are "high self-monitors"; that is, they continually monitor their own social performance, adjusting it instantly when they detect that they are not having the desired effect on other people.

Certain professions, Snyder points out, seem to attract people who are adept at this type of impression-management:

> Professional actors, as well as many of the more mercurial trial lawyers, are among the best at it. So too are many successful salespeople, diplomats, and politicians.

These "high self-monitors" can be easily spotted because they habitually exhibit the following key traits:

- They read social cues expertly, paying careful attention to others, scrutinizing the tiniest nuances of expression so as to know what is expected of them before speaking or acting.
- They try to imitate the people they would like to be with, and they even try to make people they really dislike think that they are friendly with them.
- They modify their appearance in different fashions, as the sociological situation dictates, rather than simply "being themselves."

As for the leopard, he (or she) cares little about what anyone else thinks. Obviously, for most of us, the chameleon is a lot easier to get along with in those first minutes of meeting than the leopard. Their perceptions cause lightning reactions. The chameleon fits in immediately; there is rapport established instantly.

Trouble looms when chameleon and leopard meet each other. Psychologists point out that then conversation lags, expressions cloud, vibrations become jangled and intense. There is little communication and what there is becomes difficult.

Part Chameleon . . .

Those champions among us, like Lee Iacocca again, are a bit of this and a bit of that, with the ability to turn on each facet quickly and with expert timing.

Iacocca can be chameleon as well as leopard. When he was selling cars in the South as a young man, he had a standard ploy he used in order to make himself fit in with the people of the South. Obviously his crazy name, which was actually Lido Iacocca, made him out to be somebody from as far away as outer space, at least.

On the road he switched his names around and changed "Lido" to "Lee." He would start out his sales speeches by pointing out that he had a very funny first name. It was "Iacocca," and he carefully pronounced it. But his family name was easier: Lee! And *that,* of course, was a magic name below the Mason-Dixon line.

> They loved it [Iacocca wrote]. I started every meeting with that line, and they'd go wild. . . . Suddenly I was accepted as a good ole boy.

. . . and Part Leopard

But he could also be the opposite. He could be every bit as much leopard à la John Wayne as anybody else could be. His favorite words were those of any ruthless commander:

> Okay, I've heard everybody. Now here's what we're *really* going to do.

WHEN HONESTY BECOMES QUESTIONABLE

While honesty and accuracy are important in establishing yourself in any relationship, as can be seen from the preceding discussion on chameleons and leopards, there is a level of self-disclosure that should not be passed in the first moments of a business relationship. Honesty is important, but it should be tempered by a definite vagueness. In fact, it is best to be *very* vague in establishing a friendship with a stranger, much in the way the chameleon simply does not ever reveal its *true* color.

I want to go back to my original conversation with my Fortune 500 appointment in the restaurant.

"I'm sorry I'm late."
"That's perfectly all right."

Suppose the conversation were being held between two other people—not between me and the CEO. The latecomer continues to speak even after the diner accepts his excuse. He has a compulsion to elaborate:

> "I was held up by a dentist appointment. I had a ravaging toothache. I think it's a kind of guilt feeling stemming from a fight with my ex-wife. When I got to the dentist's office I discovered that he was at Bellevue. His son had been hurt in a car accident. His receptionist was in tears."

Wow! This is a living soap opera! But even then the latecomer does not stop.

> "She referred me to another dentist down the street. I told him I had a bad toothache and asked him to check my teeth. He cleaned them instead. I just got back to the office in time to find that my secretary was out because the radiators had burst in her apartment and she had gone to meet the plumber. I'm going to fire her anyway, but wouldn't you know she was out on a day like this?"

TOO MUCH TOO SOON

To put it mildly, this man's disclosures are much too self-revealing and too detailed for a first meeting. His revelation that his toothache might have resulted in guilt feeling over a fight with his ex-wife is simply not the kind of comment you expect at a first meeting.

The same is true of his revelation in regard to the dentist whose son had been hurt in a car accident. And the comment that he planned to fire his secretary simply is not something to have with lunch.

And yet some people feel that they should clutter up their talk with such details. An appropriate response made to cover the man's lateness might simply have been exactly what I told my Fortune 500 lunch companion:

"There were a number of complications at the office."

My point about vagueness is not lightly taken. The details of the toothache, the dentist appointment, the teeth cleaning, and the secretary's problem—all are fascinating, certainly, perhaps to someone close to you. But at a luncheon where two people are engaged in the very delicate operation of becoming acquainted with each other for business purposes the story is not appropriate.

It is best in the first five minutes of any meeting to confine the subject of the conversation to impersonal things. The weather is always a good icebreaker. So is the state of the country or some big news story that is just breaking and that is not controversial. So is the atmosphere of the restaurant or the bar in which you are eating. So is the state of the business in which you are engaged, particularly if your companion is in the same business.

PRELIMINARY PREPARATIONS

You could say that the first five minutes of a meeting constitute about 1 percent what happens during those five minutes and 99 percent of what has happened to make those people what they are all through their lives.

In other words, each individual brings to any meeting with another person a tremendously assorted cultural, social, and psychological clutter of baggage. The great bulk of this material is involved in preliminary preparation. It can be broken down into a number of important elements:

- Verbal language
- Nonverbal language
- Grooming
- Listening ability
- Psychological motivation

- Charisma
- Perception
- Enthusiasm
- Emotional control
- Physical control

When it is all put together, however, the result becomes the motivating force that drives you to arouse interest and respect in another person—all during those crucial five minutes.

I'D ALWAYS LIKED TO BE . . .

In looking back over successful interviews that I have had with people, I realize that either consciously or unconsciously I have always been trying to project a specific image of myself to the people I meet. In that effort I am certainly not alone, and I believe that what I am trying to convey is pretty much what you would want to convey, too.

Although many facets of character and image are abstractions, they do get across the central idea that I am trying to project. Let me put down a series of words one by one so that you can see them and think about them.

- Authority
- Certainty
- Consideration
- Credibility
- Empathy
- Inspiration
- Integrity
- Intimacy
- Luster
- Presence
- Resolution
- Self-assurance
- Understanding
- Vigor
- Vivacity

All these particular character traits are facets of the cut stone that could easily become the special image that you wish to project. I am going to discuss each facet for a moment to show you why it is important in reflecting a part of your basic self—the self that will become effective in putting you over in those first five minutes of meeting.

Authority. Everyone wants to be in control. The ability to lead others attracts people to you. If you project authority, you are on the right track toward impressing people.

Certainty. Honest belief in a fact, an idea, or a concept can inspire others to feel the same way. Steadfastness is definitely a builder of corresponding understanding and empathy between two people.

Consideration. No man (or woman) can be an island unto himself (or herself). He or she must be a part of the human race. It is this facet of personality that brings an individual closer to all other individuals.

Credibility. No matter who you are or what you are involved in, you must be able to project a feeling of belief in other people. If you cannot, or if your belief can be questioned, you will not arouse belief in yourself or in your hopes.

Empathy. Empathy is more than compassion. Compassion is the ability to feel the way others feel. Empathy is the capacity to put yourself inside another person's skin and experience feelings and emotions directly.

Inspiration. Your own passion projects excitement into other people. This is one of the most important facets of a person's general profile. It is the ability to arouse others to a purpose or project.

Integrity. The pretender is usually unmasked after a short time together with the nonpretender. Without integrity, you cannot convince anyone that you are going to do what you say you are going to do.

Intimacy. This is the vital link between two people that makes them much more than two separate individuals. This is the final involvement of two people, usually in an ongoing business relationship.

Luster. In the presence of a person with inner glow, your own doubts and hesitation thaw. It is a force of energy that can bring people together to work in concert for whatever the individual wants.

Presence. Presence is the force of personality that makes everyone in the room look at you when you enter. It is the essential ingredient in the actor or actress and in the politician. It is "being on."

Resolution. Without resolution, a person cannot channel his or her energies to release vital inner forces that will make others want to carry out work-force objectives with enthusiasm and vigor.

Self-assurance. The person who projects a feeling of self-assurance will attract support and assistance from underlings on the job as well as superiors. There is a steadying influence on everyone associated with a person possessing this vital quality.

Understanding. To lead others you must be able to intuit their feelings and emotions and be able to sympathize with their hurts and wounds. Understanding builds a bond between coworkers that is difficult to break.

Vigor. This is a person's magic core which is able to release energy and the force of personality on associates everywhere. It is what fuels all action and endeavor, all positive thought, all progress, and all the important things in life.

Vivacity. If you have the ability to express through vivacity your own excitement and enthusiasm, you can usually get others excited about what you are doing, about yourself in general, and about the work you want done.

HOW TO CREATE AN IMAGE

Of course, these facets of character are the ones I have decided on over the years, but I find them truly effective in projecting the real me. Since everyone is different, with different goals and different perceptions of self, these particular facets of character may not do for others or for you.

The idea is for you to make up your own list of effective facets of character. List them, study them, see what they mean, see if you can honestly apply them to yourself, and then continue to relate to them and let them shine through in the image you project to the world.

Remember that if you impress these ideas on your mind so that they are always there inside you, you will gradually *become* a person who projects each of these scintillating character facets in everything you do.

2

SAYING IT RIGHT

A great deal of the ability to project the proper business image depends on a person's skill at speaking effectively. When I say "effectively," I mean speaking in such a manner as to achieve clear, crisp, relaxed, and thoughtful verbal communication.

To effectuate such successful verbal communication, it is necessary not only to be able to control exactly *what* you say, but *how* you say it.

What you say is based on your own general outlook, the purpose of meeting with the person you have chosen to meet, and a large number of other factors in your makeup. What you say depends a great deal on prior preparation, forethought, and other bits of effectively performed homework.

How you say it depends on personal habits of verbalization, including emotional attitude, tone of voice, accent, speech patterns, volume, pitch, pacing, phrasing, projection, and a complete absence of verbal tics or affectations.

THINK BEFORE YOU SPEAK

Before going into any particular elements of speech—all of which can be worked on and improved with practice—I want to discuss a most important point.

Communication in speech is a two-way street. The Shakespearean soliloquy is a stage convention that does not exist in real

19

business life today. A person who stands on the street corner talking to no one in particular will be thought to be seriously in need of help by passersby.

Therefore, verbal speech is dependent always on a listener or communicant. Except for the initial statement made to open up a dialogue, every piece of communication involving speech is a direct reaction or response to *another* thought expressed in speech.

Note: Speech is *not* a series of isolated thoughts. In speech, statement is linked *absolutely* to prior statement. In addition, speech is linked absolutely to thought.

If I were to remind you to "think before you speak," you would smile benignly and shake your head at my naïveté. Nevertheless, this is one of the most important keys to effective speaking in the business world. It is so obvious that you probably forgot all about it after you left grammar school.

THINGS TO LOOK OUT FOR

There are several typical flaws that develop in speech if you do not think about exactly what you are saying at all times. These flaws include muddy logic, imprecise ideas, ungrammatical utterances, interruptions, nonsequitors, and unrelated ideas, among other errors.

The urge to interrupt the person you are talking to is one of the worst habits you can fall into. Once again, this is usually a result of opening your mouth before you form your thoughts. Quite soon you will annoy the person so much so that the conversation will roll over on its back and die.

Besides interruptions, you can easily kill the entire point of a serious business discussion by uttering some piece of nonsense that has nothing to do with the subject at hand. Once linkage is destroyed in verbal communication the entire process of statement and response is jeopardized. There is no *reason* to continue, and any business rapport you may have wished to establish is lost forever.

It is usually possible to do something about the bad habit of speaking without thinking by concentrating on what the other person is saying and following the line of thought being communicated. In turn, you can then reply to that line of thought with consistency and intelligence, and succeed in building a bridge to a common business understanding.

CARE AND THOUGHT IN COMMUNICATION

Most of the bad habits of verbal speech—speaking too quickly, speaking in a high-pitched voice, speaking too loudly, and speaking ungrammatically—can be corrected by making sure of what you want to say before you open your mouth.

By listening carefully to your business associate, you symbolically take a deep breath before saying a word. If you take your time to speak, you will offend no one.

Item: It is not the person who takes his or her time during communication who is annoying; it is the person who prevents anyone else from speech who causes others to clam up and drop out of the conversation.

Item: It is the careful, slow speaker that everybody listens to, not the quick starter who is usually full of half-baked ideas. Business communication is based on care and thought. Effective marketplace give-and-take can be ruined by lack of attention and concentration.

HOW TO COMMUNICATE VERBALLY

As for the actual elements of verbal speech, I have found that the following four key precepts differentiate good speech habits from bad ones.

1. Clear diction
2. Slow speech
3. Low pitch
4. Relaxed attitude

1. The Key to Clear Diction

Clarity of diction is without doubt the most important element in good verbal communication. I have noticed that most people in business as well as elsewhere tend to speak carelessly, slurring their consonants and uttering their vowels without precision. A lot of the trouble stems from bad habits picked up when they learned to speak as a child.

You learn to speak by listening to others. Your first efforts at vocalization depend strictly on imitation. You pick up good habits or bad habits from those close around you: your parents, your relatives, your neighbors, your peer group.

Naturally you are also influenced by the particular regional accent spoken by the larger group that makes up your relatives, your neighbors, and the people in your general community. Not every American speaks the same way every other American speaks. Boston and Cape Cod accents are notorious: President John F. Kennedy never said "Cuba" the way most other Americans said it. He called it "Cuber." Most Harvard graduates neglect the two *r*'s in the name and call their institution "Hahvahd."

A Good Accent Dies Slowly. Comedians on television and in night clubs have a field day with the various regional accents in America, although the differences are being slowly ironed out by the ubiquitousness of television. Nevertheless, accents die hard. Although most television sitcoms are made either in New York or California, the native New Yorker can be easily spotted when he or she speaks in rich, big-city accents. Southerners also maintain their regional twang; so do Texans.

In addition to regional accents, ethnic groups that originally spoke languages other than English tend to have accents that seem unusual to an ear attuned to standard American speech. Accents, reinforced by a community, can linger on for years in people who think they have lost them.

There is a lot to be said for a regional or ethnic accent. It can make an otherwise dull person somewhat more interesting. It is rumored, but by no means certain, that Henry Kissinger has retained his heavy Germanic accent through choice. His brother, I understand, speaks without a trace. But Kissinger has got a lot of good mileage out of his gutteral spaced-out accent. His utterances assume a grandiose and ponderous weightiness that make them seem more authoritative than they would be if spoken in a normal way. That accent also makes anecdotes about him much more easily told and easily remembered.

A Little Clam in the Chowder.   Such an accent may come in handy on special occasions. I knew a friend who had always tried to conceal his accent. He felt that it was far too Bostonian to help him in his work in New York City. He spent a lot of time shaping up his *r*'s and rounding them off in words that had none.

He was looking for a job in New York at one time and went in to be interviewed by an older man. When he began speaking to his potential employer, he heard the unmistakable sounds of his own Boston accent before he had tried to stamp it out.

Eventually, as the interview continued and the rapport between the two of them seemed to be well established, he broke off.

"You know, you sound exactly like some of my relatives in Lynn, Massachusetts. Have you ever been there?"

"Been there? I was *born* there! I lived there for years before coming to New York."

It turned out the two of them had mutual acquaintances, and the talk continued on a more personal and intimate basis. He did not get the job, but he was able to get a lead to another potential employer who did hire him.

Needless to say, as he continued talking to his new found friend from Lynn, he began to regain his old Massachusetts accent.

What Style Do You Want to Project?   Actors and actresses know the value of an accent and build diction tricks into their speech to achieve special effects. It all depends on how you want to treat an accent. If you are trying to build up a particular type of personality, do it in whatever way you want to. If you are ashamed of a particular background and want to rise above it, try to eliminate the accent that labels it. For every rule that says an accentless speech is best there *are* exceptions. It all depends on your own individual image and the proper style you want to project.

Nevertheless, I do want to point out one thing. In business it is generally best to cultivate a bland, flat, and unaffected style of diction. A professional businessperson is not a professional actor or actress who deliberately cultivates speech patterns that may be bizarre, cute, or memorable. Professional businesspeople deliberately try to remain in low profile, with little indication of their geographic origins, ethnic background, or social status—if any.

In business, take it from me: Humdrum is best.

What is worse than an accent in the business world is a speech pattern that is the result of just plain laziness and sloppiness. If you have grown up around people with bad speech habits, you will be bound to have bad habits, too, not only in your grammar but in your diction. You may even have picked up numerous bad habits simply by speaking too quickly or too lazily. After all, if everyone around you has understood you for years, why try to clean up your act?

The point is, you *must* clean up your act if it is bad or you will never succed in the competitive, exacting, and demanding world of business.

2. Slow Speech Is Good Speech

Try speaking in front of a mirror now to see if you are indulging in lazy and sloppy speech habits. Speak any sentence in a natural way, exactly the way you usually say it. But this time watch yourself as you speak.

You will probably see that you speak swiftly and carelessly, with your words tumbling out in an unclear fashion and your phrases falling all over one another.

If this is the case, you know that you need help.

In the unlikely event that you find yourself speaking clearly and distinctly, slowly and thoughtfully, skip the rest of this section and go on to the next.

The likelihood is that you are talking too fast and do need help. And if that is the case, continue your vigil in front of the mirror and speak in exactly the opposite manner. Speak the same sentence you spoke before, but this time speak it slowly and carefully, looking at your mouth as it forms the words and making sure that the words are shaped carefully and deliberately.

Make sure that each sound you want to say comes out in the way you want it to come out. You can achieve this by slowing down your speech patterns with cool deliberation. Pronounce each syllable; that is, pronounce each syllable that you *should* speak. Some consonants and letters in English words should *not* be pronounced at all. If you are unsure, a glance at a dictionary will show you what sounds to voice and what sounds not to voice.

Fast Is Not Always Best.   It is a general rule that most people speak in a natural way much faster than they should speak. This is especially true of urban Americans. The natural swift pace of the busy city tends to speed up actions of all kinds, including speech.

The conversation between two excited friends who meet on the sidewalk after months of estrangement can become almost unintelligible to anyone within hearing range.

Think about it a moment. If you have ever tried to study a foreign language by listening to people speak that tongue at a normal rate of speed, you will understand the difficulty. Normal speech for an urbanite is probably *twice* as rapid as it should be.

Therefore it is always a good idea to enter into a communications relationship with a new business acquaintance by assuming that you *are* speaking too rapidly. Never forget: By speaking at a more sedate pace, you can get your thoughts across more clearly and more easily.

Let's assume that you have analyzed yourself in front of the mirror and have found that you talk too fast. One way to slow yourself down is to time yourself as you talk. At first you will feel that you are dragging your words out and making yourself nervous by hesitating.

Disabuse yourself. No one ever really bothers to criticize a speaker who is too slow. It is the speaker who is too fast who becomes a problem to the listener.

By deliberately dragging out your words you will find that you have acquired a new dimension to your diction, a dimension that affords you a kind of confidence, authority, and conviction that you may have completely lacked before.

This new aura of confidence and authority is certainly one step in the right direction toward the total businesslike impression you are trying to create in the person you are communicating with.

3. It's All in the Pitch

When William Shakespeare wanted to characterize a woman in a positive, loving sense, he wrote:

> Her voice was ever soft,
> Gentle and low, an excellent thing in woman.

Thus he wrote when he penned lines for King Lear who was speaking about his daughter Cordelia. For the moment let's forget about what happened to *her*. The point in Lear's speech is well taken. His comments could be posited by a speech therapist today. Those key words are: *soft, gentle,* and *low.*

Your voice is an instrument, exactly like an oboe, a cello, or a violin. It can perform a number of very difficult functions. It can be used to make music, to recite poetry, or to play a role on the stage. And it can be used to communicate intimately, persuasively, sharply, or deliberately. It can also be used to communicate angrily, testily, insultingly, or hysterically.

The major area in which the human voice can be misused is in its pitch. The playwright recognized the efficacy of speaking in a low pitch—soft and gentle. Many people believe, however, that no one pays any attention to them unless they speak in a high, strident voice, with words uttered by a tense, tight throat.

I suppose this is the natural way in which an embattled individual tries to frighten off an attacker. A woman screaming for help when she is being assaulted uses her voice to save her life. Her throat is tight, she is nervous, she wants to project terror, and her tone is pitched high. This sound is calculated to bring help from far off.

Any animal is able to produce shrill sounds in combat or in flight or in terror.

Getting the Voice Pitch Down.   For a situation of dire peril, a shrill, high-pitched diction is proper. But for a business situation, one in which you are trying to impress someone else with your rationality, your integrity, your self-confidence, and your innate good taste and judgment, you do not want to emit the tones of a shrike in distress.

Fear is *never* the emotion to portray or arouse in a business meeting of any kind. If you allow fear to leak out in your actions, in your diction, or in your words you have lost ground that cannot be recovered. If you inadvertently arouse fear in the person you are discussing business with, you have lost the battle completely. The *opposite* of fear—confidence—makes for good business relations.

Fear is a no-no. Fear kills.

You *can* cure the problem of a high-pitched, fear-betraying, or fear-arousing voice, once you discover that it exists. The trouble is, many people do not even *know* that they are pitching their voices too high. If you have spoken that way all your life, and if no one has pointed out to you that your tones are hurting his or her ears, you may think that your high-pitched diction is normal. Well, it may be normal for you. But others will find it offensive—others who have never met you and who are going to meet you tomorrow at an important business conference.

How will you affect *them?*

Obviously, in a negative way.

And so you must change this bad habit.

There are various ways you can gain control of the pitch of your voice. One of the most important is to remember one thing. If fear and hysteria cause the voice to rise, you must never allow yourself to fall prey to fear or hysteria when you are in a business meeting.

In other words, if excitement makes the voice rise, keep your excitement under control. Lack of excitement makes the voice lower. It is better to relax and avoid excitement of any kind than allow it to enter any encounter. If you can relax, then you have won half the battle.

Remember: The key to low-pitched diction is relaxation.

It's Not Easy to Relax.   The ability to relax is not an easily acquired habit. Usually, when you are going to meet someone for the first time to discuss business, you tend to tighten up. You want above all to impress your new contact. You want your image to come across in the best possible manner. You want to elicit a positive response in this person who may help you make a solid sale, cut a good contract, or simply bring in new business to your firm.

You must learn to control any nervousness that is liable to

creep into your actions, and especially, you must keep its presence out of your voice. If you are keyed up, you tend to tremble or perspire. If you are keyed up, your speech tends to speed up and to soar upward.

The most important thing to learn to keep your voice down and your diction clear is to relax and let your vocal chords assume a more natural tension. Relaxation is the key to total voice control. If you are calm, you can control the pitch of your voice, its speed, and—more important—even the subject of your speech.

The Too-soft Voice.   Although it is quite rare, you may have learned to speak in a too-soft voice, one that cannot be heard normally by anyone else sitting in the same office. If so, you will find that you are probably self-conscious, fearful, and lack confidence. Once these psychological difficulties are cleared up, your voice will return to normal.

The point about the too-soft voice is that vocalization is not necessarily the answer to the problem. It may have to do with your overall psychological configuration. As such, the problem will be solved once the psychological situation is resolved, and certainly not until all such complications are resolved.

The Too-loud Voice.   Although the usual stereotype of the Texas windbag is a person who talks too loudly and swings his or her arms when speaking, other people who are not Texans sometimes speak too loudly to people around them. If you are guilty of yelling at close range, you may not even be aware of it. You may even be a bit hard of hearing and not know it. But because your friends know you they will probably accept the fact without telling you about it.

Loud speech can also be caused by feelings of inferiority. The Texan I just mentioned comes to mind. Braggadocio is usually connected with feelings of inferiority. The braggart speaks more loudly than anyone else to make his or her voice heard above all others. The person who feels less effective than anyone else around will certainly try to project an image of superiority by giving the impression of self-satisfaction and confidence.

Verbal Tics and Crutches.   As you try to clean up your verbal act, you should take careful aim at your own diction and zero in on habitual phrases you use, extra words you throw in to give yourself time to think, and any number of "crutches" used to pad out your speech.

One of the most common tics in speech is the use of the long, drawn-out "uhh" or "ahh"—however you spell it.

> "It gives me great—uhh—pleasure and—uhh—a sense of—uhh—pride to introduce Mr.—uhh—Johnson—uhh—to you today. His—uhh—credentials are of the utmost—uhh—are impeccable. For seven—uhh—years he was chief executive—uhh—officer of . . ."

This is a disastrous habit, because it is something that you do not hear yourself doing. You have to make an audio tape of yourself in order to catch it. Most people are amazed when they hear themselves doing the "uhh" routine.

Once spotted, it is relatively easy to cure. You simply make an effort *not* to say "uhh" when you are pausing to think of the next words to say. The pause will be attributed to exactly what its cause is—a thinking space. Not only is an honest pause of clear air better than the "uhh," but clear air also tends to make what comes after the pause that much more weighty and *important*.

Like Wow!—You Know?   The second-most common type of tic is the currently popular phrase "you know," which two generations have inserted in almost every sentence uttered since the year 1960.

> "I was in the middle of a—you know—very *boring* air trip to Chicago—you know—on the fast jet from Kennedy Airport—you know—sitting next to this Lee Iacocca type—*he* thought—you know. Now this guy had a—you know—*drinking* problem, but he claimed to be a—you know—world-class salesman."

The "you know" crutch has no reason for existence. If you assume the person to whom you are communicating already *knows* what you are about to say, there is no point in speaking. The obvious answer to the phrase—when it is used to extremes—is as follows:

"No, I *don't* know! Why not tell me?"

During the "you know" period of the sixties, another crutch word—"like"—surfaced as a vogue utterance too. I think it is on its way out, but it occasionally surfaces even today where it is least expected.

"Like I was at this—like—*conference* of unutterably *dull* engineer types—like—last year, and there was—like *nobody!*—I could rap with—like on a peer level. It was like—yuk!"

Hack, Kaff, Kerflubb, Harrumph!   Another and disastrous type of verbal tic is the unnerving habit some speakers have of clearing the throat just before uttering a word. You can become a victim of throat clearing because you are nervous; in this case the throat clearing is used for a purpose. However, whether or not it is necessary or simply habitual, it is irritating and should be avoided at all costs.

A more or less specialized type of verbal tic is the regional habit of ending a sentence with a rise in pitch—making a statement seem to be a question. Listen to yourself ask a question like: "Is it too late to try?" Your voice goes up on "try." That makes the sentence a question rather than a declaration.

On the other hand, some people have an ingrained habit of ending *every* sentence with a rising inflection. "I'm going shopping at the supermarket." Said with a rising inflection on the last word, the statement shifts into an equivocal and quasi-questioning mode rather than a declarative one.

The Proper Mood for the White House.   A speech therapist was once monitoring President Jimmy Carter during his stint at the White House. She found that he was delivering his most important points in a kind of halting, questioning manner—typically the fashion of the soft-spoken Southern gentleman.

"Let your voice go down at the end of the phrases you want to emphasize," she instructed him.

Carter was astonished. "They told me to go up to emphasize!"

The therapist smiled and delivered herself of this rather telling evaluation:

> "Fourscoure and seven years ago? Our forefathers brought forth on this continent? A nation? Conceived in liberty? And dedicated to the proposition that all men are created— equal?"

Carter got the point. His voice began to go down at the ends of his phrases, and he gained a great deal in credibility.

4. How to Relax

One of the easiest ways to try to relax your throat is to yawn deliberately. Close your eyes and let your jaw drop loosely on your chest. This is the right position to initiate a yawn. Let the yawn take over, opening your mouth and the back of your throat as wide as possible. Feel the way your throat muscles stretch out.

Your throat should be open when you speak. To test out how your throat functions, say a series of "ah's," while looking in the mirror. You'll notice that the uvula pulls up. (*Uvula,* incidentally, is Latin for tiny grape. The uvula *does* resemble a tiny bunch of grapes hanging down there in your throat. See it and recognize it.)

Now say a series of "ng-ah's." On the "ng" sound, you will note that your throat is completely closed. On the "ah," however, it will be completely open.

Relax your tongue. Let your head hang loosely on your neck. Look in the mirror. Try to ease all tension out of your tongue, letting it rest slackly. It's not easy to do; the tongue pulls back, humps up, trembles.

Do the best you can.

Fa La La La La, La La La La.   You know the old Christmas song "Deck the Halls"—the one that winds up with a lot of "la's." It is not necessary to sing it. Just speak it. Say "la la" the way you do around the wassail bowl. A singer uses the same sound in order to relax the throat muscles before starting a scale exercise. It is not a bad trick to remember. You will find the tension begin to drain away from your tongue and throat the more "la la's" you utter.

And there's always the groan drill. Open your mouth. Put your tongue between your lower lip and your front teeth, and let it loll there, relaxed. Groan deeply, directing the sound up out of your throat to your tongue's tip. Let the groan get outside your mouth.

Next, lower your jaw loosely, chin touching your chest. Let your tongue hang out of your mouth. Speak through your open mouth, breathing out the alphabet for four letters, and breathing in the alphabet for four more:

> While breathing in: *A, B, C, D.*
> While breathing out: *E, F, G, H.*
> While breathing in: *I, J, K, L.*
> While breathing out: *M, N, O, P.*

And so on. Do not pause between breathing in and breathing out. If you do so you will soon be going to sleep. But keep the flow constant. When you begin to yawn—and I guarantee you *will* yawn!—let the yawn take over, and keep your head down.

In fact, let your head hang down on your chest. Close your eyes and count slowly to ten. Then lift your head from its sagging position, open your eyes slowly, and look at the ceiling. Try this exercise several times. You should experience a diminishing of tension.

Now let your head hang down on your chest again. Then roll your head from one side to the other. Do this over and over again. Then let your head sag downward in front, hanging there loosely. You will begin to feel the tension going away.

Better lock the office door while you do these exercises. People might begin talking.

Achieving Effective Speech.   Let me emphasize once more that relaxation does a lot of good to your speech. If you are minimally tense when you speak, your speaking voice will be more effective than if you are very tense. Your voice will be deeper and more resonant, your words more clearly spoken. You will be able to manage a great deal more variety in your voice with a much wider range of volume and better breath control. The total effect will be a more controlled and persuasive manner—the very image you want to project in any business situation.

Opposed to the good that relaxation does for you in improving your speech, tension builds a wall between you and the person with whom you wish to communicate and whom you hope to influence. It tends to shut down warmth and ease; it builds up coldness and distance, which is exactly what you do *not* want when you are trying to sell someone an idea or a product.

Clearing the Throat Is a No-No.   The act of clearing your throat tends to strain your vocal chords. In turn, clearing your throat too much can make you hoarse. Hoarseness results from extreme tension, which makes your throat muscles too tight to produce normal speech.

Try this exercise to reduce the need to clear your throat:

- Yawn until you feel that your throat is completely open.
- Relax your mouth and your tongue in the manner described earlier.
- Pretend you are a dog and begin to pant low and slow, making the sounds in your throat.
- With your mouth relaxed and your tongue limp, inhale and exhale noisily.
- Let the air move over your tongue, down your windpipe, and then back up again.
- Cause the air to blow the phlegm off your vocal chords.

This exercise tends to dry out the throat. Make sure to swallow after you do the exercise five times. You should repeat the exercise at least ten times; then you should rest and repeat it in an hour or so if you feel you need to.

LIST OF GOOD SPEECH HABITS

Here is a tip sheet for you to memorize. Actually there is no need to commit it to memory word for word, but remember the main points. These are important tips on what to do and what not to do when you speak with anyone during any kind of business meeting—formal or informal.

If you learn these points and practice them regularly, I guarantee you will improve your conversational ability in a dramatic way, and in a very short time.

Try it and see.

Stop, look, listen—and then speak! Pause a long time before you open your mouth to speak in front of your business associates. Let everyone else see that you are thinking. This will give them the impression that you have control over what you have heard and that you are about to impart some intelligent feedback on the subject. Speak when the suspense is at its peak. The pause makes whatever you say more serious than it would be if you blurted it out. The pause helps *underline* the importance of what you say.

Consistency is the key to speaking well. It is unbusinesslike to be inconsistent. You must learn to be consistent when you speak to your colleagues. Even in a conversation that is informal, you must not change your mind in midsentence. Remember that, contrary to what you may have thought, *all* speaking is *public* speaking. When you are talking to another person, even during a coffee break at the office, you are speaking in public. Never let your speech degenerate into sloppiness or thoughtlessness or triteness. Keep it on a tight leash.

Speak softly and be heard further. I learned a trick of speech from one of my English professors years ago in college. When he would hear students mumbling in the back of the lecture hall, he would deliberately lower his own voice almost to a whisper. And, believe it or not, you could really hear a pin drop. He knew that the soft voice is the one everyone tunes in to. Marlon

Brando pulled that trick in *The Godfather*. If it's good enough for Brando . . .

Always speak the truth about yourself. You may choose to lie sometimes when you are talking to someone; there are all kinds of reasons to do so in the game of business conversation. But always speak the truth about yourself. If you fail to tell the truth about yourself, your own body and body language may give you away. Do not *pretend* or try to cover up something about yourself. The old admonition of the 1960s still pertains today: "Let it all hang out."

Speak formally and avoid contempt. Familiarity, especially in business speech, certainly does breed contempt. When you are speaking in a businesslike way, keep your diction as formal as you possibly can. You can make a pretense at informality by your manner, but never let your diction lapse from the precise and the accurate. Informality tends to make your grammar and diction sloppy. Never allow this to happen. Sharpness and clarity of speech will make your image businesslike and crisp.

Listening is the first step in speaking. Be sure you learn to listen as you continue to learn to speak. The more you listen, the more ammunition you will acquire with which to speak, and the more ways you will learn how to express yourself persuasively and project the kind of business image you want to. When you listen, listen creatively, working along with the colleague who speaks so that you can almost guess what words he or she will say next.

Don't try to be amusing—it's not funny! Telling bad jokes is probably the easiest way to turn most people away from you when a serious discussion is under way. Leave humor to the professionals. It is the one way to ruin an otherwise impressive performance as a person with good commercial and business sense. Somerset Maugham, a witty man himself who understood the proper usage of humor, once warned a friend:

Don't make people laugh. If you do, they'll think you're trivial.

Avoid obscenity like the plague. One of the worst of habits is that of swearing and larding speech with all the four-letter words known to the human race. During the 1960s, four-letter words became the rage in intellectual circles, particularly within college walls. By now they have crept out from academia until you hear them even in the office or at lunch. I am positive that obscenity will someday be on its way out. Avoid it at all costs. It is a bad habit once acquired, and it is hard or perhaps impossible to shake. But it offends people—even people you might not expect to be offended. Not everyone is as liberated as you have been led to believe.

Avoid euphemisms like the plague. Another thing to avoid at all costs is the use of euphemisms. This advice may seem to contradict the previous advice about obscenity, but actually it does not. You must avoid both. Call a spade a spade; call a table leg a leg; call a breast a breast. Euphemisms appear around us every day. They are invented to obscure speech, to avoid offense, to deaden pain. Sometimes pain should be tolerated. Simply use the proper term for what you talk about. A garbage collector is not a sanitary engineer; he or she is a garbage collector.

Avoid slang, jargon, and gobbledegook. One of the most difficult jobs anyone has these days is reading bureaucratic pamphlets or news releases. Nevertheless, business, education, the clergy, the law, medicine—almost *all* areas of endeavor—manufacture jargon day after day, some without even realizing it. As a writer and phrasemaker, always go for the real word, not the jargon that masks it from view and pretends it is something that it is *not*.

In short, say it right, say it short, and say it well.

3

SUCCESS IS LISTENING

Although it was not particularly a smashing surprise to anyone with normal perception in business, the discovery made by the Rand Corporation of California some time ago was a revelation of dramatic proportions to the intellectual community:

Nobody listens!

It took hundreds of close studies to determine that committees composed of some of the most brilliant minds in the business world generally produced the most banal and ineffective reports in the history of communication.

The reason?

You are right. Because nobody *ever* listens!

WHAT THE RAND STUDY FOUND

The study found that each member of a typical control committee was so eager to be heard that he or she never bothered to listen to what any of the others in the group were saying during their turns at bat. Each was rehearsing a personal message so energetically that no thought was ever given to what anyone *else* was saying.

The same situation is frequently true of an ordinary conversation between two people who are closely related in an in-house business situation. How many times have you been brought up short by the plaintive cry of your secretary or your bookkeeper:

"You're not *listening* to me!"

And, what is more, you probably have to admit that indeed you have *not* been listening. You have been moving ahead in your own mind, assuming that the conversation is going in a certain direction and you can always catch up with it later. But somehow it has changed course and you find yourself all alone out there somewhere on another side track that is not switched into the main line at all.

LISTENING IS AN ART FORM

Half of the skill of conversation is the ability to listen. It is more than an ability; it is an art. The cleverest conversationalist is usually not the one who says the most words and holds the stage for the longest time, but the person who listens the most carefully and is able to make a particularly trenchant comment at a crucial moment. *That* person is the one remembered, not the monotonous monologuist whose train of thought has been seized upon, studied, and reduced to a pithy statement, and by that rarest of all conversationalists, the *listener!*

One of the most important elements in business communication of any kind is mutual understanding. Mutual understanding is impossible without an occasional shifting of point of view. That is, you must trade positions with the person with whom you are communicating to see things the way he or she sees them.

IT'S ALL IN THE POINT OF VIEW

Try a little experiment in communication when you are away from the office milieu. Watch carefully the next time you are at the movies or looking at television. You will note that a scene starts with the camera focused on someone doing something or saying something. Before the scene is played out, the camera cuts to *another* person, showing what that person thinks or how he or she responds to the action or statement originally made.

In film parlance, this is called a "reaction shot." What it *really* does is show the way the act or statement made impinges on *another* character. It is essentially an instantaneous shift in point of view. But its importance is not in its swiftness or its inevitability; It is in the dramatic evaluation of how the sayer or doer affects someone else. In short, it is simply the dramatist's trick in showing how communication is *accomplished*.

It is the same in all communication. You must put yourself in the other person's shoes for the moment in order to understand that person's feelings, thoughts, or ideas. This act requires imagination and mental agility. Without imagining what the other person thinks or feels, you do not really involve yourself in true communication.

If the other person does not trade places with you when you are explaining your own idea, he or she will not be involved in communication either. The trick of mutual understanding—the purpose of communication—is in being able to shift your point of view with facility and with accuracy.

You have to be able not only to be in your own shoes and say what you are saying, but you must be able to put yourself in the other person's shoes and evaluate what you are saying in his or her way.

LISTENING VERSUS HEARING

A lot of the success of such understanding relies on the communicator's ability to make the other person—the communicant—see things exactly as the communicator sees them. The easiest thing to see through another's eyes is a visual scene. That is the value of good storytelling technique: The communicator relies on anecdotes, with the anecdotes bringing the idea alive to the communicant.

This is all by way of getting at the principal point—the value of *listening*. To listen is to do a great deal more than simply to hear. People *hear* many things: the beep of an automobile horn, the scream of a siren, the creak of the stairs, the hum of the electric typewriter. Most of these sounds are relegated to the dustbin of the subconscious because they do not signify important or relevant things.

The Magic Tapestry of Sound

To *listen* is to put together all the sounds you hear and assemble them into a picture in your mind's eye. Through sounds you hear, you can form a picture of something you have never seen yourself. If you listen carefully, you can hear a great number of sounds; in your mind you can put them together and form a brilliant picture of what is happening *out of your sight*. You can weave a magnificent tapestry that becomes rich and strange by combining the clues afforded by your ears and the wit of your imagination.

On a more mundane level, you listen for the sound of the computer printer to ascertain that your copy is ready to be torn off the machine. You listen for the sound of the coffee wagon to signal the morning coffee break. You listen for the sound of the buzzer that calls the executives to the conference.

By assembling the sounds you hear into a picture outside yourself, you are performing the important skill of *active* listening. Active listening is, in turn, the key to mutual understanding, which I mentioned earlier.

THE OTHER WORLD OF COMMUNICATION

By imagining sights communicated through the words of another person, you can put together a picture that is the same as that seen by the other person. The complicated picture you assemble is the essence of pure communication.

You can actually leave your own world, become a part of the world of your communicator, and live that person's experience along with him or her. To do so, you move from your own point of view to your communicator's point of view. This is a magical journey that enables you to be somewhere you have never been before, to see things you have never seen, to experience vicarious feelings you have never felt.

The key to vital communication is your own desire to come to know the person with whom you are in communication: to understand, to see the world through other eyes, to think the way another is thinking. The key to this type of interrelationship is your ability to listen actively to whatever he or she has to say and to re-create what is being conveyed through words in your own reconstructed images and emotional pictures.

It takes work to listen creatively. It takes effort, but when you do manage to listen creatively, you establish a bridge between yourself and your communicator that becomes a two-way avenue of understanding. You become more alive by sharing your communicator's feelings and imaginings; your communicator becomes more alive by being able to lead you into that other world.

So many people cut off any chance of communication by tuning out when someone is talking to them in order to rehearse what they are going to say when it comes their turn that it is hard to believe *any* communication can ever be effected. For, once the bond of communication is severed, it is difficult ever to reestablish it.

It is like the suspension bridge in Thornton Wilder's novel, *The Bridge of San Luis Rey*. Once the main ropes snap, the bridge and all the people on it are doomed to destruction at the bottom of the canyon below, never to be resurrected again.

Planks in the Bridge of Communication

Whenever you listen to anyone else speak, you should always keep one question at the back of your mind:

"What do those words mean to this person?"

Words are planks in the bridge of communication. But words have different shades of meaning to different people. What one word means to you may mean something else to the person with whom you are in the act of communicating.

By keeping in mind this essential difference, you remind yourself that you are listening to another person who is unique and who sees the world in an individual way that is different from yours. You are trying to understand the thoughts and feelings experienced by that person by carefully following his words and phrases and absorbing their meaning.

Creative listening allows you to help the other person put together whatever the message is. Emotions are difficult to put into words. Unlike a conversation between two people discussing substantial things like foreign locales or construction techniques, a conversation may occur between two people that deals only in emotion.

When such a communication is established, it is likely that the communicant may try to help the communicator put those complex ideas and feelings into proper words for articulation. The creative listener helps as much as possible.

"I don't quite know what you're saying. Can you put it into other words? Do you mean something like this . . . ?"

The Use of Feedback

In the case of a complicated communication such as one involved with a discussion of emotions and feelings—for example, a conversation having to do with habitual lateness, improper attitudes on the job, or a drinking or drug problem—the key to a successful communication is patience. As communicant, you listen to the communicator carefully, rephrase what that person says, and try to put it into words that both of you can understand.

Not all listening is as difficult as that between a troubled person and a supportive friend, or that between a superior who must discipline or terminate a subordinate. In fact, most communication in business is not difficult at all, but is a great deal of fun. It is fun, however, only if you actively participate in it, and do not let yourself shut off the flow of input as you try to prepare your own feedback, without knowing what the feedback is feeding on!

Listening is not a passive activity. Unless your mind and persona are involved, you are not really listening at all. You are just hearing sounds.

Reaching Out to Touch Someone

It is your job to reach out and catch exactly what is in the mind of the person speaking to you. A good listener, an active listener, should never be distracted by a speaker's mannerisms or tone of voice. The *intentions* of the speaker are what is important. You must always remember that what the speaker is trying to impart to you is what you want to know.

I have mentioned how you can help the speaker if the words do not seem to be building a proper bridge between the two of you. It is as important not to accept thoughts that are imperfectly fashioned as it is not to accept words about feelings that do not pinpoint the true emotions under discussion.

In other words, even if your conversation has nothing to do with a troubled person, you should make sure both of you are on the same verbal wavelength before you agree with anything that is said.

The Importance of Good Feedback

Communication involves give-and-take. What I have just mentioned—the active involvement of the communicator and the communicant—is an important part of creative listening. Using computer terminology, it becomes active feedback.

The Legitimacy of Communication

Consider yourself the listener, and your communicator the speaker. You are performing active listening. Your communicator is a thinking, feeling person. You may not necessarily agree with what the speaker is saying, but you *do* acknowledge the legitimacy of the communication by a remark or two.

These remarks, forming an effective response, are what constitute feedback. Feedback is reaction that goes back to the speaker as assurance that he or she accounts for something, not because of *what* is said, but because the speaker is involved in communication.

Without some kind of valid feedback from you, to show that you are actively participating in the communication, the speaker might easily feel put down and invalidated as an individual. To sit there and listen without displaying a shade of emotion or making any indication that you are *hearing* what is said is to make the speaker feel nonexistent.

Such a conversation would gradually slide to a halt. The only option for the speaker in such a case is to quit talking and disappear.

Between Communicator and Communicant

Effective feedback starts with a commitment between speaker and listener, a commitment in believing that both individuals amount to something, that neither is any better than the other, that it is natural that both be open and honest with one another. Working from this hypothesis, there are all kinds of wonderful results that can be obtained by interaction between these two conversing persons.

Feedback is a response to another person, the act of speaking directly in response to a statement or question, meeting the speaker where he or she is. Feedback requires creative listening to be valid. Its meaning is important: You have heard what the speaker is saying and you understand. There may be details, however, that are not quite clear. Feedback in response is usually given as a request for some kind of clarification or evaluation. It is also used to correct errors that might have crept into the transmission of the information from one to the other.

You can look on feedback as a means of monitoring the communication bond. The purpose is to double-check the effectiveness of the communication and to assure that the correct meaning is shared.

Descriptive versus Evaluative Feedback

Feedback can be descriptive, or it can be evaluative. However, no judgments should be made, no labels pinned. The listener should simply clarify what the speaker has said without adding argumentation or persuasive elaboration. The listener should not project any judgment about a statement. The pinning of a label can be regarded only as a hostile response that can put the speaker into a defensive posture. Such a reaction must be avoided.

To be effective, good feedback:

Must be specific. You should never pull any punches or try to evade the truth. Feedback should avoid vagueness and ambiguity. Your response should be narrow in scope, and it should focus exactly on what the speaker says, not on what the speaker might have said or could have said.

Must be immediate. Feedback should never be after the fact. If it is not immediate, the bond of communication between speaker and listener will be broken. If it is not immediate, the actual thought tends to blur in the distance of time.

Must be directed toward feelings and actions. These feelings and actions must be controllable as opposed to considerations that are beyond control.

Must never be commiserative or sympathetic. Feedback should never offer any kind of help. If it does sympathize, feedback becomes a kind of wailing-wall technique of stroking that gets the speaker nowhere.

Must be a simple link in conversation. Feedback should be part of creative listening that assures the speaker that the listener knows where the conversation has come to, where it is going, and understands it. It should be a statement in reverse that assures the speaker that both communicator and communicant are in sync and are ready for the next step in the communicative process.

RULES TO IMPROVE THE LISTENING PROCESS

There are several important rules to follow to improve your performance in creative listening. They are fundamental precepts in any kind of communication between people. Nevertheless, it is amazing how much these precepts are ignored or deliberately sidestepped.

They are divided into three main areas:

1. Visual contact
2. Verbal interruption
3. Imposition of meaning

1. Visual Contact

You must always look at the person with whom you are communicating. For effective linkup, you should always look at the person squarely and directly. Visual contact is not only important when you yourself are speaking but also when the other person is speaking as well.

Visual contact is the best way to establish a bond between you and your communicant. You should continue to work solidly on this connection once it is established. Without it, you will lose contact or will diminish the communicatory bond and lose all the positive gains established to bring your business association to a successful conclusion.

Note: Do not stare at the person with whom you are communicating. Look at the person and let him or her know that you are there all the time the act of communication is going on.

I was recently at an important cocktail party in Beverly Hills, standing and talking with a West Coast businessman of some note. He was directly in front of me, and my back was to the wall. The rest of the room spread out behind him. Our conversation continued animatedly, and then suddenly he interrupted what he was saying to shake his head and laugh.

I was slightly disconcerted and asked him what had broken his train of thought.

He said:

"Absolutely nothing is the matter. I can't help noticing how different you are. You're facing this enormous room with hundreds of celebrities in it. Almost every person here is a household name. But since we've been talking, your eyes haven't once stopped looking at me. I can't help but be flattered by your attention."

I considered that a compliment, and I report it as such. Remember that you have to listen not just with your ears, but with your eyes as well. If you fail to look the speaker in the eyes, you will never know what thought or idea he or she may be trying to communicate to you. The eyes can say a lot.

2. Verbal Interruption

Just because a person stops talking does not necessarily mean that the conversation is over. You must let a speaker have time to think something out. A pause may mean that your communicant is gathering thoughts or mentally formulating meanings.

I am simply warning you not to feel that a moment of silence in a conversation is a bad thing. With continuous dialogue and snappy comebacks a staple of television sitcoms, many Americans have the wrong idea about true conversation. To a television producer, one moment of dead air is a sin. To the average person, one moment of dead air is actually a moment to rest and recuperate; it is a moment to savor and think ahead.

Do not try to fill up an interruption when you are in conversation with someone by the immediate interjection of a statement of your own. You may be killing an entire thought process on the part of your fellow conversationalist. Worse than that, you may be in the process of making an important sale and inadvertently lose it by breaking your prospect's concentration. Or the person with whom you are conversing may be at a crucial point in the difficult resolution of a problem. By your interruption, you may kill an approach beneficial to you.

Clearing All the Hurdles.   As a creative listener, you must consider yourself as an important part of another colleague's revelatory process. People reveal themselves in fits and starts. I have heard this process compared to a runner who jumps a series of hurdles. By getting over one hurdle, the runner establishes a stride and can then go over another and another, and so on to the end.

As the speaker encounters and clears each hurdle, the problem or intricate resolution of a problem becomes more and more revealed. The speaker makes each succeeding statement more complete with difficult details. The runner is testing out the ability to jump these hurdles; the speaker is likewise testing abilities and keeps going over higher and higher rails.

Help your communicant along. Never try to stop him or her.

It is that last hurdle that lets the speaker open up to you. If your conversation is a complex commercial one, this last step will be the most difficult and, to you, perhaps, the most rewarding.

3. Imposition of Meaning

Each individual faces feelings and thoughts that no one else experiences. It is quite difficult to express some feelings, particularly emotional ones that may occur in business dealings as well as in others. You should never allow yourself to place value judgments on another person's innermost thoughts.

It is not necessary to agree with everything another person says. You can argue or discuss any point at length. But a good listener—a creative listener—never expresses value judgments like the following:

- "You can't mean that!"
- "You're never going to be able to sell the boss on *that!*"
- "Why did you ever let yourself get caught in an old salesman's trap like that?"
- "He's a sloppy dresser and a fuzzy thinker. You know he can only make the company look bad."
- "That was the stupidest thing you could have done! Why did you move her into the typing pool?"
- "Putting Jack on the road is the silliest thing I ever heard of! We'll never see him again!"

The creative listener avoids such put-downs and value judgments in favor of statements that acknowledge the speaker's feelings and then invite objective discussion.

About Value Judgments and Labels—Don't! I cannot stress too strongly the fact that value judgments are a very destructive force in normal conversation. A value judgment is an instant label. A label is a stereotype. People are individuals, no matter how easily they may *seem* to fall into specific categories.

I also think of a label as a serious detriment when you apply it to yourself. That is, if you think even secretly of yourself as a loser, you will *be* a loser. If you think of yourself as possessing an inferiority complex, you will *have* an inferiority complex. If you think of yourself as a difficult person, you will *be* a difficult person.

What labels do to people is to categorize them and put them into a specific box. It is a most difficult job to get them out once they are packed neatly in place.

Think Small—Be Small.   I knew a man who wanted to go into business for himself. He was an intelligent and personable individual. He loved books. He wanted to sell them in a store. But for some reason he had an idea that a small store in a shabby corner would be better than a big store in a bright spot. In short, he was dreaming small; he was thinking small; he was living small.

He opened his bookstore in a small way; he purchased his books in a small way; and he ran his business in a small way. Of course he failed. He went into the business to fail. He had put a label on himself that categorized him as a "little guy."

You simply cannot succeed if you think of yourself as a "little guy." Even if you are a little guy, and eventually succeed as a little guy, you would be better off if you went into the game of business and played it as a "big guy" to win big—or at least as a guy who wanted to succeed.

There is an ancient joke:

Man: I lost my collar button.
Wife: Where did you drop it?
Man: Over by the bureau.
Wife: Then why in the love of heaven are you looking for it in the corner?
Man: There's more light over here.

What have both those stories to do with creative listening? Plenty. Both have to do with individuals who are deliberately going into a situation to lose. The little guy with the bookstore labeled himself a loser, and sure enough he lost. The guy with the collar button on the floor labeled himself a loser, and sure enough he lost.

Watch out for labels. The man who failed with the bookstore had labeled himself *small,* in a pejorative sense. The man with the lost collar button had labeled himself as *deprived.* Not a good idea, in either case. The individual had decided it was impossible to win. Both had placed the wrong value labels on themselves and ruined their chances.

I am reminded of the popular song titled "I Gotta Be Me." For some reason, the singer of the song, the "I" person of the lyrics, has labeled himself or herself as someone who is being pushed around by life. The thrust of the lyrics and the idea behind the song is that the singer is desperately determined to *be* himself or herself no matter *who* tries to interfere.

The big climax of the song comes in the recitation of the title line:

"I gotta be me!"

The disk jockey played the song through one morning, complete with its ending belted out in typical show biz tradition. He then paused after it was all done and came on in a soft and casual tone of voice:

"So who's stopping you?"

In listening and responding to someone else who is speaking, watch out for value judgments, labels, and snide remarks.

- Never judge.
- Never give a verdict.
- Never pass sentence.

It will be *you* who is imprisoned in the end.

LISTENING IS NOT A SPECTATOR SPORT

I think I should clarify one point. I have been discussing listening in such detail that I may have misstated one overall concept. Even though I called attention to the difference between the verb "hear" and the verb "listen," I would like to restate it.

- To hear is to be aware of a sound.
- To listen is to hear with thoughtful attention.

Creative listening is *not*—repeat, not—a spectator sport. I say this because a large number of people born into the television age think of listening as being seated in front of a video screen and watching and listening to what goes on there. This is *not* creative listening. It is spectating.

In the novel *Being There*, Jerzy Kosinski satirized the phenomenon of the total spectator. His hero, Chance, had no ideas of his own, no thoughts in his head. Chance simply watched television from the day he was born until he was thrown out into the real world when his protector died.

Because his world was the video screen, he perceived the real world as being a part of that same video screen. Since he had never been forced to respond or to act on his own, he simply *watched* what went on.

Through a series of quirks he eventually became a consultant to the president of the United States, and later appeared headed for the oval office himself. He rose quickly and dramatically to the heights of power because he simply repeated what he had seen and heard and did not involve himself in any kind of original feedback. He *reflected* what any person said to him and wished to hear.

The secret of Chance's success was that he was the ultimate chameleon, able to become the mirror image of everyone whom he encountered. Because he was the mirror image, he reflected back what was fed to him without change or alteration of any kind. He *seemed* the most original and brilliant man in the world because all other people saw themselves in him and liked what they saw.

It was a funny idea, a funny book.

Think about the spectator concept when you are listening to someone communicate with you. Active listening involves *real* thinking and *real* reacting. You must remember that the communication bridge does not go in one direction only; it is a two-way route to better understanding.

A one-way route leads to the strange world of Chance that Kosinski was satirizing in his unnerving book. True creative listening leads to effective success in business and in influencing people who count.

4

CREATING A
PRESENCE

The key word to describe the "right" kind of person to strike up a proper deal with is "businesslike." The dictionary definition for "businesslike" is simplicity itself:

Efficient, practical, or realistic.

In fact, any *other* kind of person—the unbusinesslike person— is definitely unwelcome in most business circles. With the shedding of the three-piece suit in the 1960s cultural revolution, it looked for a while as if shirts and ties would never come back.

But they did.

Efficiency, practicality, and realism have returned as well. Today's climate in business circles is definitely back on track. The main concern of anyone entering the business arena is to look businesslike and to act in a businesslike manner.

And that includes how that person carries himself or herself, how he or she acts and moves from a standpoint of nonverbal language as well as the manner in which he or she dresses. For the moment, I want to concentrate not on the outer lineaments of the image, but more specifically on the inner resources.

SPEAKING WITH THE BODY

Any modern study of communication must inevitably involve an analysis of nonverbal language, popularly called "body language."

In an integrated personality, nonverbal language is the complement of verbal language. In a personality susceptible to confusing emotional contradictions or if a person is not telling the truth for some reason, verbal and nonverbal language battle with one another. The manifestation of the struggle sometimes unmasks the individual's real intentions.

For the person involved in business today, it is mandatory to understand how to read body language and how to put it to use in influencing others. It is also vital for the person to make sure that he or she can control his or her own body language to prevent any misunderstanding by others.

Body language is basically a counterpart of verbal language. To understand body language, it is first necessary to understand verbal language and how it developed through the ages.

Talking Doesn't Make It So

Verbal language, which started out in prehistory as an attempt to communicate true feelings between individuals, has unfortunately come to be used not only for telling the truth but also for imparting the lie. Words that once were utilized to put together a true picture can now be employed to put together an untrue picture.

The politician with his or her bloated promises extended out to his or her constituents is the image stereotype that leaps immediately to mind.

But there are many people other than politicians who use words to confuse; and many of them are involved in business and commercial ventures. For example:

- Salespersons
- Real estate agents
- Insurance agents
- Physicians

And there are a whole raft of others. Listen, for example, to these words of wisdom from Ralph Waldo Emerson:

What you are speaks so loudly, I can't hear what you say.

Emerson had the ability to listen with both ears and watch with both eyes to mark the contradictions between speech and action.

So did the writer of the following Biblical sentence in Proverbs:

> He winketh with his eyes, he speaketh with his feet, he teacheth with his finger.

The Absence of Credibility

Obviously if you can spot the contradictions in a person's verbal language and nonverbal language, you are not going to give the person good marks for credibility. In fact, incongruous gestures and faulty blending of verbal and nonverbal gestures tend to turn everyone off completely, and rightly so. If there is the slightest suspicion that a person is using contradictory verbal and nonverbal gestures, that person is probably in the midst of perpetrating some kind of falsehood. Generally speaking, it is natural for verbal and nonverbal gestures to coincide, to blend smoothly together to impart a picture of serenity and probity.

Yet, like all sweeping generalities, this statement is not completely true either. Some people simply do not manage to get themselves together with enough skill to be in sync with their personas. Their images are imperfect—a little blurred at the edges, a bit out of focus, a bit double-visioned.

It is the person whose instincts are not *quite* right who becomes negatively affected by the inability to blend verbal and nonverbal into a clear picture of credibility and naturalness.

The Importance of Physical Presence

When a good actor walks on the stage, his or her presence commands attention even before the actor opens his or her mouth to speak. The actor has mastered the ability to project presence, presence communicated by bodily intensity. This type of physical intensity is created by a proper contracting of the muscles of the body so that the entire organism is poised, ready to—well, swing at a golf ball or swat at a baseball.

I am not saying that you should always stand as if you were at attention in front of a regiment of marines. I am simply saying that stage presence has a great deal to do with an actor's ability to hold him- or herself correctly and project his or her persona to an audience as an entity totally in control of itself.

Of all body language, it is *bearing* that communicates presence the most quickly and effectively. Generally speaking, bad posture does more to make you look a wreck than bags under the eyes. Sloppy sitting, slumped standing, weary walking—all communicate age and ugliness. Slouching in a standing position or slouching in a chair—both are bad marks for you. The message you send out is always interpreted:

"Does it *really* matter?"

The Lost Art of Pantomime

In a way, it is unfortunate that motion pictures developed the ability to project sound and became talking pictures. When they simply showed movement they concentrated on body language to the exclusion of all other language. A good actor in the silent era could make you believe anything he or she wanted to. Communication from the screen to the audience was accomplished strictly by means of body language.

The gestures, of course, were exaggerated, but they were specific and communicable. When sound came in, when dialogue became part of the film scene, the whole tone of motion pictures changed. The art of pantomime vanished.

And yet the more practiced star understands even today that both verbal and nonverbal language are a part of the artist's bag of tricks. With a speech expressing rage and madness, the actor makes all movements underline the rage and madness of the speech. With a speech expressing love, the actor makes all movements show ardor and passion.

When Verbal and Nonverbal Clash

On the other hand, by fractionating verbal and nonverbal language—that is, by combining one nonverbal gesture with a verbal statement to the opposite effect—the actor manages to produce laughter. The disparity between verbal and nonverbal is always enough to make the audience giggle.

Often enough the disparity is not sufficient to cause the audience to react to it properly. Sometimes the disparity is quite subtle, and indicates only a character's inability to project a single impression successfully. This is the kind of bad body language that you should always try to avoid. It can lead only to negative reactions from the business colleagues with whom you are communicating.

The trick is for you to learn to keep your nonverbal gestures completely in sync with your verbal statements. Only in that way can you be sure to project the image you want to.

BEING TALL IN THE SADDLE

The most important images you want to project on the business scene are those of confidence, of authority, and of conviction. You can start to achieve them by practicing your posture. You should be able to demonstrate authority and command either from a standing or sitting position.

You can learn to be tall in the saddle by standing with your head and chin up, your rib cage high, your stomach tucked in, and your body held together in total intensity.

Standing. When you are standing, push your head up as high as you can, until you can *feel* it stretching. Then let your shoulders slump as if you were trying to lift a heavy weight from the floor. Keep your weight evenly distributed on your feet.

Sitting. When you are sitting, pull yourself up tall in the saddle, keeping the top of your head as high as you can. Pull your head up even higher, as tall as you can go. Let your upper body bend slightly forward.

An Air of Authority and Confidence

These are the two basic positions for Tall in the Saddle. You can actually give yourself an air of authority when you meet someone else if you stand that way and sit that way during conversation.

Walk tall, shake hands, then choose a straight-backed chair for yourself. When you sit, keep your chest up and your upper body tilted forward. Let only the lower part of your spine touch the chair back.

A good listening position. Tall in the saddle is an excellent posture in which to listen creatively. Sitting back in a passive position makes you look slumped and inert. By projecting your upper body toward the speaker, you are thrusting yourself actively into the scene where the action is.

A good nonfatiguing position. Oddly enough, tall in the saddle keeps down fatigue and exhaustion, too. Carrying your head high on top of your spine is easier than letting it sag. You'll also feel about twenty pounds lighter.

A good lightweight position. Just to check it out, let yourself slump after you sit tall in the saddle. See? Your body is heavier already. By standing and sitting tall you will project authority, confidence, and conviction.

GESTURES AND MOVEMENTS

Now let's take a look at other elements of body language. These all come under the heading of gestures and movements. Although there are many nuances and tics that I want to take up later, you should note that there are two ways that most people move about:

Smoothly and slowly
or
jerkily and swiftly.

In speaking and in moving about, a relaxed, responsive, and easy series of movements tends to project an attitude that puts everyone else at ease. It is even easier for you to listen creatively if you are in a relaxed attitude. It is easier to smile, easier to nod acquiescence, easier to move about in a chair or behind a desk.

To anyone watching you, movements you make that are up-tight, tense, and jerky can be off-putting. Out-of-sync gestures and rapid-fire sentences tend to upset anyone trying to make sense out of them. Erratic movements telegraph bad news to the person watching you; the message is that you are nervous, tense, and *worried*. Such an attitude in turn evokes only a negative response: suspicion or distrust.

Seek Out Your Natural Style

Perfecting your bodily movements are primarily a concern of your growing-up years. By the time you reach adulthood, you have developed and shaped your natural style. Everyone does this, whether he or she knows it or not. It is always best to stick basically to that style no matter what small changes you might decide to make in it later.

If you *do* discover that your natural way is to move in jerky spasms and speak in rushes of words, simply slow down the speed and try to smooth out the rough edges. Do not attempt to re-create your whole personality. Re-create only parts; never tackle the whole.

If your natural style is to be voluble and to move your hands and body as you speak, do not try to change yourself totally *now*. Years ago it was not the "in" thing to accompany verbal language with body language. Today, however, there is nothing wrong with using your hands or your shoulders to underline what you are saying in verbal language.

In fact, the person who does not use the hands at all, who tends to play the great stone face, who is totally inscrutable, is the one who is not considered the norm on today's scene. Styles change. It's not hard to change with them.

Psychologists are convinced today that the person who is up-tight, who does not let his or her hands move, who keeps his or her face in a frozen deadpan, is tense, nervous, and *disturbed*. Such a personal attitude projects tension, coldness, arrogance, and even distaste to others. It is an attitude that immediately sends out warning bells to anyone who beholds it.

Today the relaxed manner is in. The stiff manner is out.

WHAT NERVES, TICS, AND TWITCHES MEAN

An anthropologist named Desmond Morris has studied a number of people, examining them to see if they exhibit nonverbal signs of nervousness when they are engaged in telling lies. He conducted the experiments by making his control subjects tell lies deliberately at certain times and the truth at others. His findings are interesting.

He discovered that in telling lies, the two easiest expressions to control are

the voice
and
the face.

He discovered that one of the hardest nonverbal expressions to control is

the body.

Lying, he found, causes a person to fidget and move about nervously in the chair. Moving about nervously also involves touching various parts of the body—the nose and the mouth, for example—while speaking.

The control subjects sometimes scratch their wrists, rub their shoulders, or toss their hair about through their fingers. Some even scratch their noses; swing their legs; twirl pens and pencils; fiddle with jewelry; scratch their heads; tap their fingers; play with their glasses, pens, or papers; rub their noses; scrape their chins; fold and unfold their hands endlessly; or indicate tension in dozens of other ways.

Tension and Prevarication

While Morris's experiments concerned lying, the same manifestations occur when individuals are under tension for one reason or another. They, too, tend to fidget like the control subjects instructed to prevaricate.

To prevent people from thinking you are lying, it is best to try to suppress fidgets that, rightly or wrongly, give the impression to others that you are up to no good.

One way to stop your hands from fumbling about is to dig your nails into your palms. The pain elicited should stop you.

An important lesson to be learned from a study of body language is that of consistency versus inconsistency. I have already mentioned contradictory messages: a message of contempt and distaste in nonverbal language and a message of approval and applause in verbal language. That is inconsistency on a large scale. It is a message to the recipient that you do *not* really approve of him or her, but are simply *pretending* to do so.

RULES OF BODY LANGUAGE

That brings up another important point. What exactly *are* the rules of body language? Are they the same for everyone? If so, why is there no set of rules available so that actors and individuals interested in body language can study them?

Here is what Edmund T. Hall, an authority on nonverbal language, says about that:

> Because of its complexity, efforts to isolate out "bits" of nonverbal communication and generalize from them in isolation are doomed to failure. Book titles such as *How to Read a Person Like a Book* are thoroughly misleading, doubly so because they are designed to satisfy the public's need for highly specific answers to complex questions for which there are no simple answers.

One of the most obvious nonverbal manifestations is the tendency of an individual to lean toward someone who is liked and to lean away from someone not liked. Another obvious body language sign is the habit of a person fearful of bodily harm or physical abuse to sit hunched up in a defensive posture. Another is the action of an angry man in grabbing hold of the jacket lapels of someone he wants to threaten or challenge.

Obviously, if a burly man grabs you by the jacket lapels and shouts at you, "In my humble opinion, sir!" he is *not* being sincere.

He is resorting to jungle tactics in nonverbal language and pretending civility in verbal language. Body language is the language to believe. The rest—the voice, for example—can be manipulated and shammed.

Says Hank Calero, a consultant on nonverbal communication:

> If a man tells you he has an open mind on the subject, and at the same time he clasps his hands, you can be confident that his mind is already made up.

What Do You Really Think?

There are dead giveaways that reveal how a person *really* thinks. For example, if a person peers over his or her glasses or tilts the head down to look at you, he or she is obviously suspicious of what you are saying. And, in the same vein, the person who constantly nods his or her head at everything you say is not really signalling agreement at all, but is revealing deep skepticism.

In his studies, Morris found that a man who rubs his nose when you talk to him is not simply satisfying an itch, he is expressing reservations about what you are telling him, or about what he himself is saying. When a person brings his or her fingers together to form a steeple, that is a worldwide gesture of supreme confidence; in other words, the person who steeples his or her fingers in front of you knows he or she is one up on you, so watch out!

Not all such gestures are universal. Many of them are identified geographically, which makes it difficult if not downright confusing to try to create a dictionary of universal nonverbal language.

- An American will exhale when he is angry or in any way frustrated. A Japanese, on the other hand, will suck air to demonstrate the same emotion.
- In Vietnam, a person always uses one finger to beckon an animal—but only an animal. In America, a person uses a finger to beckon a person as well.
- In Japan, you should never sit down and cross your legs. It is considered an insult to show the sole of your shoe.

- The gesture of the rounded thumb and forefinger—the okay sign—*is* okay in America, but in Latin America it is an obscenity!

TRAFFIC ON A TWO-WAY STREET

Like all communication, body language is a two-way street. Once you have succeeded in lining up your verbal and nonverbal statements so that they coincide at all times and reinforce one another rather than contradict, then you may be sure that you are projecting the proper image for whatever business point you are making.

At the same time, you must remember to analyze the verbal and nonverbal signals coming from the person with whom you are doing business. As I have said, scientists believe that body language actually has a far greater effect in displaying a person's real thoughts and feelings than verbal language does.

How much greater?

The ballpark figure is a one-to-four breakdown. That is, verbal language involves only about 20 percent of the total "language" expression, leaving a good 80 percent to nonverbal statement.

I was skeptical of this breakdown at first, but when I began studying people who came in to see me in the office, who were circulating at office parties, who were taking part in business discussions, I realized that indeed what the psychologists said *was* true. A good actress onstage, for example, underlines her image and the thoughts and feelings she wants to project about four times as much with her body and her movements as she does with her voice speaking the lines.

WHY ACTING IS CALLED "ACTING"

The theater has always depended for most of its magic in communicating excitement to the audience not on the lines that are spoken—although they play an integral part in the underpinnings of drama, reinforcing the story line—but on the "acting" of the people involved. To act is to pantomime emotions, ideas, and thoughts. To speak is simply to articulate.

As I sat in the theater one night it came to me that a person in a theater audience will watch carefully for any clue an actor or actress may give to dramatize a character's inner emotions. The twist of a shoulder, the casual flip of a hand, an arched eyebrow, a tilt of the head; every one of these movements always *means* something to the viewer. When a good actor underlines his words in order to build up a double-edged attack, then his dramatic power is intensified by the support of both verbal and nonverbal dramatic language. When the cold stare belies the warm words spoken at the behest of the dramatist, the effect aroused is one of obvious hilarity; the audience *knows* the character is emanating hostility and pretending to project affection. The audience *sees* the contradiction and is amused at the transparent deception.

And yet, I thought, most people who are amused at the effect of such disparities in the theater are not able to translate their ability to view an artificial production into an ability to work a real-life scene and spot the incongruities that abound in everyday life as well as on the stage.

The Living Theater of Conversation

It takes study. Think of life as living theater. The next time you meet someone new in a business situation, take time out to study the person to whom you are speaking, not to impress him or her with your own wit and sparkle, but to watch and match (if such is the case) the verbal and nonverbal language.

Study further: Try to match up the person's clothing with his or her total image. See if there are discrepancies. Quite possibly there are some, perhaps not many. Most people do not really get their act totally together before they take it on the road. Many are still working on it as they run through their tryouts. It really takes your best effort to get an act together that will finally make it to Broadway.

Nonverbal communication moves even further out from verbal communication when it extends beyond the persona of the individual in question. I have already mentioned clothing and how it is used to reinforce the image projected by verbal and body language. It goes even further. Note that a person's office or living room in turn reflects elements of the persona, so that not only the voice, the face, the body, the clothes, and the movements of the person become part of him or her, but the controlled environment as well.

The Story of Henry

Not long ago I was involved with a personable businessman I shall call Henry. Henry had finished college in the 1960s and was pretty much a product of that era. He was what I read to be a definitely people-oriented person. He spoke in a well-modulated voice, he directed his thoughts outward, and he did not crowd in on himself. He was an outgoing, warm human being.

Henry was a very low-profile person. He did not overreact nor did he overassert. He always maintained good eye contact when he spoke with me. That is, he did not search out celebrities in a dining room or pretend to be personally involved with the headwaiter while talking with me.

He wore informal clothes, a bit too colorful for my taste, but certainly in keeping with the warm image he had established for himself. At times he played it cool. He modified his tailoring to the mood. But he tended toward warmer colors than colder ones.

His letters were nicely informal, with just enough slang and bounce to make them fun to read. He was a personnel manager for a large appliance-manufacturing company headquartered in New York City. He was good with people. I knew that he had been in personnel work from the beginning of his working life.

A New Career in Mind.   Our association continued for some time after we met at a sales conference. One day Henry took me to lunch and confessed that he had decided he was going to get out of the appliance-manufacturing business and try to go it alone. What he wanted to do was to set up a personnel agency. He knew he was good at working with people and could succeed at the job.

He needed a backer. He said he did not have the money to make a go of it all by himself. He had managed to put aside a fairly large amount of money, but he needed a pretty big nest egg to make the new firm fly. He knew that I had just made a fairly large chunk of money on a venture and wondered if I wanted to take a gamble on him.

I am always suspicious when people come to me offering me a chance at a good thing, particularly when I am the one who has to put up the money. I was suspicious of Henry now, as well. But I knew him pretty well by that time. I knew that he was a low-key person, a man who seemed to be oriented to people. I had never checked up on him at his office, because I had no reason to. After all, I had met him in the company of several associates of mine. I did not usually run security checks like a C.I.A. officer.

Before we parted at lunch, Henry invited me out to his home in the suburbs. He lived in Westchester County, New York, up near the Connecticut border. He was married and had two children. I got his address and drove up to see him at the allotted time.

A Surprising Nonverbal Statement.   I don't know what I really had in mind, but the house in which Henry lived stunned me. It was built in futuristic design, all square angles and straight lines, with an enormous amount of glass and aluminum set into heavy wood paneling. It overlooked a small lake. The living room was high-ceilinged with a huge expanse of glass along one wall, looking out into the woods.

The furniture was clean-lined and metallic, the kind of stuff you might see in a science-fiction movie. Henry and his wife and kids seemed to rattle around in the place. For some reason, the house did not really *go* with Henry.

After an excellent meal, during which I met his wife—who was charming and warm, quite the right mate for Henry—I finally said, "I'm curious, Henry. Is this your place on a permanent basis? Or do you simply rent here temporarily?"

He shook his head emphatically. "I designed it," he told me with a sense of pride. "I've always wanted to live in a house like this!"

He looked around him with a possessive smile.

The Other Man inside Henry.   We talked about the money he would need to open up his personnel agency, and I departed for the city. Something was disturbing me. The following week I managed a discreet check on Henry. He did have the money set aside that he had described to me. But he was not quite so successful at his job as I had thought he was. I spoke with one of his colleagues, a man who had worked at the company but who had departed.

"Henry's sharp," he told me. "He'll make a million in time. The only thing he doesn't like is people."

"But his whole personality . . ."

"He's acting," said his friend. "Believe me, he hates people. *Really*. He's a throwback to the 1960s. He *thinks* he's a humanitarian. He'd do better supervising production or going into accounting."

I told his friend that Henry meant to set up a personnel agency.

The friend snorted. "He'd be miserable there, just as he's miscrable where he is."

I tended to agree, now that I understood a little bit about Henry's performance on the job. Somehow I had always perceived him as typically people-oriented. I suppose I was taking him at face value, listening to and believing what he told me. I simply had not bothered to check up on him.

But it was the nonverbal statement that Henry made, particularly in his surroundings, in his environment, in the home he had designed for himself, that finally showed me the real Henry. He was a man whose verbal and nonverbal statements did not hold together without certain cracks showing.

He was essentially a split personality, although he was unaware of it because he was able to fool himself as well as almost everyone else. He had certainly fooled me. But of course he was not aware that he was fooling anyone. It was all deeply buried in his psyche.

The R and D Man

I never went in with Henry. But I did put him in touch with another acquaintance of mine who needed a good research and development manager. The last I heard, Henry was working out very well in his new capacity. He was lucky he had enough background to make that switch in careers—he had taken his minor in engineering at college.

Some people are simply not what they seem to be. In Henry's case, he did not know what he really *was*. But he had been able to construct himself to conform to a credible concept in the proper self-created mode at the time he was finishing college. But some people could read him right and they knew that he was not a person-oriented type at all.

The point I am making is that nonverbal communication goes on *outside* the person as well as inside. Be sure you check out all the avenues of such communication before making up your mind about a person.

5
DRESSING WITH CARE

A business acquaintance of mine I shall call Andy is one of the most stylish dressers I know. I use the word *stylish* and not "fashionable" to make a distinction. To be *stylish* is to dress appropriately; to be *fashionable* is to follow the trends in the fashion magazines. If you want to put it another way that makes a valid point: To be stylish is to reflect your true self; to be fashionable is to slavishly follow current fads.

Andy was not always a stylish dresser. He came from the Southwest where he had been brought up on a ranch. He wore jeans before jeans were fashionable. He hated ties and had never seen a cufflink before he came to the East Coast.

COLD WEATHER—WARM CLOTHES

His first winter in New York City was a nightmare. He had little money. He had few clothes. When the cold weather settled in, he was forced to go to a second-hand clothing store on the West Side to buy a second-hand coat.

Out of the mass of coats on sale, he found one that fit and bought it for five dollars. At least, he said, it was warm when he got into it.

However, when he finally showed it to Clarice, the young woman with whom he was living at the time, she absolutely went white with shock. Clarice was an actress, unsuccessful at that time, but trying to get a good part somewhere . . . anywhere.

"My God!" she yelped at him. "What did you buy that thing for? It looks like Dracula's cape!"

Andy was honestly puzzled. "I'm cold, that's why I bought it."

Clarice stared at him, overwhelmed by his ignorance. "You don't buy clothes to keep warm, you fool. What kind of a klutz are you?"

"All right," mumbled the mystified Andy. "What *do* you buy clothes for?"

"To make a statement about your personality!" shouted Clarice. "To project the real you!"

"Oh," said Andy.

But he learned a lesson that day. From that moment on, he began to dress to express himself rather than to cover himself up.

"You know, Clarice was right," he told me years later from a different and more mature perspective. "Your manner of dress is a message to the world about who you are and what you are. It's sometimes the only message that the world gets. Make the most of it."

CLOTHES TO HIDE BEHIND

I was thinking about Andy's adventure with that overcoat the other day as I attended a business conference in the World Trade Center in New York City. I took a quick glance around at the people who were seated near me, and I realized that most of them fell into two distinct groups.

Group 1. There were those who dressed in a special kind of uniform, an outfit to signify that they belonged to a certain professional or social class. The majority of the business executives, secretaries, clerks were in this category.

Group 2. There were those who did exactly the opposite: That is, they dressed in a way so as *not* to be recognized as belonging to any particular group. A lot of the people in this category were in the same occupations I just mentioned, except that for some reason they wanted to be considered something other than what they were.

Conclusion. What impressed me was the fact that in each case, people were dressing according to the group in which they *did* belong, either to brag about it, or to hide the fact from others.

Only an occasional individual popped out of the crowd of business people who was really expressing himself or herself as someone different from everyone else with his or her own persona, psyche, and ego. The point is, that while most of these individuals wore what the others were wearing, they seemed to wear it with a flair, to express a specific personality, or a facet or facets of a specific personality.

No matter how you may think of clothes, each time you dress you are divulging information to others about yourself. You must therefore take care to see that the statement that is going out is the message you want to send, or at least that it is composed of information you *wish* to go out.

CONSISTENCY IN DRESS

When you speak aloud you take care not to contradict yourself. Be sure to exercise the same precaution in the way you select and build your wardrobe.

Everything you wear should be of a piece. Each item of clothing should complement and elaborate on the central message you are conveying. Visual contradictions and *non sequiturs* can ruin a specific message you may be trying to develop through the selection of your apparel.

In addition, whatever you buy must accurately reflect some point or points of your personality. If it *does,* it is right for you, no matter what else you wear with it.

Quentin Crisp, a British actor of impeccable style, recently wrote:

> There is nothing wrong with high heels and blue jeans together so long as together they tell the truth about you.

In a manner similar to that in which you rehearse your speech and groom yourself in private you can likewise rehearse your dress without prying eyes watching you. All good dressers do that.

Noel Coward once said:

> I take ruthless stock of myself in the mirror before going out. A polo jumper or unfortunate tie exposes one to great danger.

What Not to Wear

There are a lot of other things that expose you to great danger in the business world. I am no expert on dress, but I do know that there are a number of things that make me grit my teeth when I see them.

To start with, I dislike a man or woman in an ill-fitting suit. There is no reason anybody today should be fitted in the wrong-size clothing. It does not cost that much to get the size right.

There is no use kidding yourself, either. Never think yourself thin if you are not actually thin. Roll with the punches: Buy fat clothes and *then* slim down. Do not buy thin clothes and promise yourself to reduce.

Another thing that annoys me is a person in clothes with bulging pockets. The worst thing you can do is walk around in a business office like a street salesperson carrying along all your wares. Put your things in a briefcase or tote bag, or stash them somewhere in your desk.

Making a Spectacle of Yourself

If you wear glasses, get the right kind of frames. They should be in proportion to the size and shape of your face. If you like heavy black frames, you may find that they tend to make you look stark. You should try to pick a color that is close to the color of your hair.

More about glasses.

- Metal frames make you look like an accountant, which is swell if you *are* an accountant, but not too good if you are an administrative manager.

- Motorcyclist frames make you look mournful. Unless mournful is your message, eschew them.
- Certain round frames make you look like a librarian. Unless you are in heavy research, avoid them.
- Dark glasses worn indoors make you out to be either a fugitive in hiding, a pussycat afraid of people, or a pretend movie star.

I do not always follow the fashions, but I do think that a person who wears out-of-date clothing is making a fool of him- or herself. That goes for hair style and length as well. You should also be sure that you are wearing the right width of tie; tie widths vary from one year to the next. Be alert. You can get away with wearing a tie that is ten years old if the styles have reverted to that width again.

A Laundry List of Beefs

Before I go on any further, I want to make out a little list of things I do not like, generally, about men and women and their grooming habits. Later on I'll go into more detail about women's clothing. Take these following pet peeves for what they are worth to you:

- Collar pins (men)
- Double-knit suits (men and women)
- Excessive perfume, cologne, or skin bracer (men and women)
- Flashy cuff links (men)
- Gold chains on hairy chests (men)
- Obvious hair coloring or hair coloring that has not been retouched in time (men and women)
- Unbuttoned shirts (men and women)
- Light-colored shoes (men)
- Loud ties (men)
- Ostentatious belt buckles (men)
- Short socks that expose the shin (men)
- Tie clips, lapel pins, stickpins (men)
- White socks (men)
- Socks (women)

THE RIGHT STUFF TO WEAR

Well, then what *is* the right kind of clothing to wear in the business world? Is it an outfit that you like? Is it an outfit that your particular job demands? Is it what your friends and peers wear? Is it what your lover or spouse likes? Your ex-wife or ex-husband? How can you select the right thing to wear and make a good impression on your business associates?

A digression follows.

A Tale of Ancient China

In old China there was an emperor who considered himself a fashion plate. He was always trying to get the "right thing to wear" in order to wow his friends and demoralize his enemies. He drove his tailors mad, ordering new outfits almost every day. They decided to teach him a lesson.

When he came in one day they said that they had discovered a brand new kind of silk and wanted to make him a suit from it. When the emperor asked to see the silk they showed it to him, but he could see nothing. They assured him it was so fine, so luxurious, that it could not be seen by the naked eye. They told him that it was very fine stuff, even if he could not see it; the very fact that he could *not* see the material proved it to be of superior quality.

He instructed them to make him a suit out of it. When the emperor visited them to see the suit, he had to admit that he could not see it at all. Even when he put it on, he was unable to see any of it.

Although he was not a particularly wise emperor, he was not totally dumb either. He said:

"If you're playing with me, I'll chop off your heads!"

Shivering, the tailors assured him that they were not conning him. They told him that he looked every inch an emperor in his new clothes.

He went out into the street to parade his new outfit before his subjects. Everyone knew the emperor's interest in fashion, and, of course, they applauded his new outfit.

"Love that jacket," one said.

"Beautiful color match," said another.

And a third: "Can't even see the seams!"

Finally the emperor came to a little boy about five years old who was standing on the street with his father, watching. The little boy gazed at the emperor for a long moment, and the emperor asked:

"How do you like my new clothes?" Now, he thought, by this boy's comment he would know if his tailors were conning him or not. And if they were, off with their heads!

The little boy turned to his father.

"Dad, I want a suit of clothes just like the emperor's!"

Moral: Never select what *you* want to wear. Let the clothes fit your image and the suit or outfit fit your job.

THE IMPORTANCE OF THAT FIRST GLANCE

Listen to some words of wisdom from Sandra Pierce, an image consultant from Westport, Connecticut, whose job it is to advise business clients on how they can look better in the marketplace.

You only get one chance for that first impression! Make the most of it.

And that's the "first impression" I have been stressing in this dissertation from the beginning. But Pierce adds more information about the importance of looking good no matter where you are or what you are up to.

Did you know that you can earn 20 percent more money, get promoted faster, do better with men and women and generally get more out of life if you improve the way you dress?

About business clothes, Pierce has a rule of thumb that is practical and should be committed to memory.

If you have to make a decision among three ho-hum suits, buy just one *dynamite* suit.

Not, of course, forgetting that the general image you should project in the business world is a tempered one, she adds:

It should be an image of dynamism and style—but in a nonthreatening, positive way.

To wrap it all up, she says,

Do the world a favor. Look as pretty or as handsome as you can!

HOW TO SHOP FOR CLOTHES

When you buy a suit, think about the message the color sends out about you. The darker the color—dark blue and dark gray—the greater the look of authority. When you are fitted for a suit, think about the message you are sending out about yourself to your business colleagues. If you are a man, make sure that you are wearing in the jacket just what you usually carry around with you: wallet, address book, handkerchief, and so on.

You think you are not partial to dark colors?

A friend of mine became a successful public relations executive after a bright career in television production. As head of his own public relations firm, he always wore dark suits that were in impeccable taste and cost a fortune. Yet he was at heart a very amusing person, with a flair for bounce and verve. Although his dress and his personality seemed to be at odds with one another, they actually were completely in sync.

But he felt sometimes that they clashed. I once overheard him exclaim to someone he had just met:

"Why do you *think* I dress in these undertaker suits? Because I'm in public relations, that's why!"

In fact, a man or woman in a service position—as a public relations executive is—*needs* to appear with authority and integrity rather than with glamour or informality. Jobs that are less service oriented call for less authority and/or dignity.

Shirts, Cuffs, and Ties

The cut of your shirt collar is very important. If you are a man and have a long neck or an Adam's apple that sticks out, you should wear a high collar to focus attention on your face and away from your Adam's apple. For a long neck, find a collar that is high in the back. For a short neck, look for one that is low in the back. Be sure the collar size is the correct measurement. A loose collar makes you look skinny. A tight collar makes you look fat. Button-down collars tend to make you look sloppy.

Your cuffs should end a little below the wrist and should be one or two inches longer than your jacket sleeve when you stretch out your arms. Have your jacket sleeve cut to fit your shirts, not vice versa. Double-button cuffs look better than singles. Short-sleeve shirts are comfortable in hot weather, but, frankly, a bare wrist makes you look like a slob.

As for ties, knitted and woven ties do not look good on a heavy man with a thick neck. The tip of the tie should usually come just to the belt buckle.

General Information for Men

You usually cannot really mess up too much if you choose to wear solid colors in your suit and shirt and a tie with a small print or a stripe. If you wear a solid-colored suit and tie and a subtle-patterned shirt, you project a good conservative image. Avoid trying to put two patterns together; they may clash. In fact, it is almost certain that they will.

General Information for Women

As for women, that is quite another story. I do not claim to be an expert on what women should wear. Certain experts have put together a number of general rules that more or less encompass a uniform look for the woman in business.

But remember that there are exceptions for every general rule. To expand your horizons a little, take a look at the following ten rules for the working woman who wants to project an image of authority.

1. Confine yourself to two or three colors in buying a basic wardrobe of coats, skirts, pants, jackets, blouses, and sweaters.

A working wardrobe could contain black, navy, gray, and beige. Combine five pieces in one color, and move these pieces around to come up with distinctively different combinations.

2. The most serviceable outfit is probably a skirt and jacket with a blouse or a dress with a jacket. And these outfits do not always have to be gray, nor does the blouse always have to be white.

3. Shoes, handbags, and briefcase should be in basic colors, too. You do not need a perfect match between shoe and bag, but the colors should be in the same family. Unusual colors are permissible in accessories like shoes or handbags, but the startling color should be matched exactly in a belt, a scarf, or a handkerchief.

4. Keep a consistency of style in your dressing. Be sure to purchase serviceable, good-quality clothes that you can mix and match in several ways. A big wardrobe of sleazy junk clothes is a waste of good money.

5. If you want a good blouse wardrobe, consider your blouse selection in much the same way a man considers his tie selection. It is in your blouse that you can have a variety of styles, textures, prints, and colors to choose from.

6. Be sure the textures you buy will properly project the image you want to show. For example, soft textures in clothing tend to give off a feeling of closeness and intimacy, inviting contact. Crisp textures indicate that you want to be regarded as efficient and independent. Clothing lines convey the same characteristics: straight and square lines, strict professionalism; curved and flowing lines, a more informal feeling approaching intimacy.

7. If you wear jewelry, keep it within limits. Gold earrings, two gold chains, or a choker, one or two gold bangles should make up the whole. If you feel that pearls suit you, they are also permissible. Be sure not to wear anything too big or too noisy. I mean *noise* in the sense of the jingle-jangle that might be generated by a charm bracelet.

8. Basic accessories are important in giving you a contemporary look in the business world. Small earrings with neat patterns

help. A watch is a useful accessory in a square, round, or oval shape with a plain gold or tailored leather band. Scarves and mufflers come in different lengths, sizes, and fabrics. You can use them to good effect.

9. Wear sheer hose, in a shade darker than your own skin or a shade that is a continuation of your skirt color. Hose should be seamless and undecorated.

10. Almost any kind of shoes are permissible today, but avoid shoes that are very bare or that have stiletto heels. These can cause physical problems. They are also noisy and tend to disturb people.

A WORD ABOUT GROOMING

The way you handle your hair, your skin, your teeth, your hands, your nails, your weight, and your cleanliness are all very much your own private affair. However, they are matters that can have an impact on your effectiveness in putting yourself across as an interesting person.

The basic thing is to keep yourself clean and neat. Shaving lotion or perfume can never cover up sloppy or careless grooming. Showering, using deodorants, and brushing your teeth are still necessary to keep yourself clean.

Most "problems" like body odor, bad breath, or dandruff are essentially matters of cleanliness, and you do not require expensive cosmetic products to avoid them. If you keep your teeth brushed and use a mouthwash, your breath should pass the test. If you bathe daily and use a deodorant, you will not have a problem with body odor. A lot of the so-called personal problems are the inspired machinations of advertising geniuses who are in business to sell certain cosmetic products.

Hair, Skin, Nails

We have come through the 1960s, with the long hair and heavy beards. Most of these excesses have vanished in the more sedate 1970s and 1980s. Nevertheless, a beard or a mustache is an attractive thing on the right person. If you are male and want to wear your hair long, keep it clean and keep it combed. Remember that it is part of your projected personality; maintain it carefully as such.

I am one person who thinks that a hairpiece is not a good idea. If you wear one to cover your baldness, you will never really know if everyone else knows you have one or does not notice. The truth is, most anyone can spot a hairpiece immediately. The problem with a hairpiece is that it is really designed to *hide* something and not *reveal* something. A person who has something to hide is usually a person with some kind of personality problem.

I tend to feel the same way about the coloring of graying hair, although a bit of discreet tinting can be done so that the touching up is not apparent at all. In which case, be sure you maintain your tint by giving your hair regular attention.

I feel, however, that if you are afflicted by baldness or gray hair, flaunt it. If you try to cover it up, everyone will know anyway. You end up making a statement about yourself in the same fashion that you make a statement about yourself in selecting the things you wear and the way you groom yourself.

Skin care can be a problem for people with conditions that make skin eruptions and scars evident. You can always get competent professional help if you feel that you have a bad complexion. The money will be well spent.

Wear your fingernails short if you are a man. Even for women, long nails can become a nasty problem in almost every walk of business life. If, as a woman, you keep your nails medium length, you will do no harm to your psyche, and you will probably be more comfortable no matter what you do.

If you bite your nails, you could be in for trouble. Most people recognize nail biting as a psychological manifestation of some deeper personal problem. You will find that most people are put off by the evidence of gnawed and bleeding nails. Try to get some help.

Once again, the way you care for yourself has a great deal to do with where you work, where you socialize, and where you spend most of your waking hours. By knowing yourself and knowing how to fit yourself into your milieu you can decide how to adapt your grooming habits to it.

How Sweet Is the Smell of Success?

You will probably wear some kind of perfume or lotion—hair oil, deodorant, or skin bracer—but you should make sure not to draw too much attention to yourself by the use of a too-powerful scent. It is distracting to have scents wafting through the air when someone is trying to make you focus attention on what he or she is saying or doing.

It is also true that certain scents are offensive to some people and actually can cause sneezing, choking, or sinus congestion.

WHO REALLY LOVES A FAT MAN?

Your weight is as much a part of you as your face, your eyes, or your total persona. Too much weight can be a definite health problem. You may need medical advice on how to control it. Besides giving you a feeling of being outlandishly huge and gawky, excessive weight tends to drain you of your vitality and energy.

However, you should always reduce under a physician's supervision. Crash weight-loss programs, fad diets, and expensive and risky weight-loss programs may harm you more than help you.

PHYSICAL ATTRACTIVENESS, OR LACK OF IT

Americans, like other peoples, have certain standards of beauty that become evident in the movie stars they admire, in the stage personalities they love, and in the television celebrities they idolize. Because beauty and good looks are epitomized so sharply in show business, many people are constantly trying to make themselves beautiful.

Question: What part does physical attractiveness play in business success? Answer: Very little.

At best, personal beauty is a silver lining on a larger cloud. If you are exceptionally handsome or beautiful, you will probably be able to make people look at you on the street or in a restaurant. You may get terrific service in a store. You will get picked up hitchhiking. You may even get off for murder in a court of law with the right people on the jury.

What It's Going to Get You

Other than that, what it's going to get you, except maybe a lot of women or a lot of men, is a lot of fuss and feathers that takes up time and energy and gets you nowhere.

It can be a handicap. You are liable to arouse a great deal of envy and mistrust in others, as well as other emotions that are impediments to your effectiveness as a business personality.

Also, physical beauty can be the cause of a lot of unwanted and sometimes dangerous sexual complications—and anyone who says that sexual complications do not exist in business situations is out-and-out crazy.

The romantic poet John Keats wrote:

A thing of beauty is a joy forever.

In spite of Keats, beauty has its drawbacks. As the saying goes, it is only skin deep. And it tends to fade quickly. In the long run, then, it is probably something that the majority of people, who do not have to worry about it because they are not burdened by it, can do without.

I think that the advantage lies with people who are less favored by nature. In other words, I think the average person has a physical advantage as the years advance and as the years make their mark on his or her face. Maturity tends to soften and to mellow the face of the less attractive.

6

GETTING DOWN TO BUSINESS

John F. Kennedy was one of the most striking examples of an individual who engendered immediate approval and trust in others. His forceful, confident, casual, and authoritative manner conveyed exactly the desired impression.

Richard Nixon, on the other hand, was often conspicuously lacking in charm and style. We often remember his churlish comment to the press after he lost the election for governor: "You won't have Richard Nixon to kick around anymore."

Kennedy summed up Nixon's manner in two succinct and devastating words: "No style."

Ernest Hemingway, one of our most famous interpreters of manner and masculine charm, summed up style as:

Grace under pressure.

WHAT DELIGHTS AND ASTONISHES

Two hundred years ago, Blaise Pascal, the famous philosopher and mathematician, noted:

When we see a natural style, we are always astonished and delighted.

Pascal had the key words well in hand—"natural" and "style." Together they combine to individualize a person. Both, projected in the right manner, cause such a person to possess "charisma," Greek for "charm."

Natural style and charisma combine to produce the magic in personal communication that makes all the bother worthwhile. It is the secret ingredient in successful business dealings. It is the *sina qua non* of getting ahead in life.

Anyone can acquire style and charisma. The only catch is that it is hard work to do it, and it requires intelligence, stamina, and good luck.

How can you acquire natural style and develop charisma?

Where Does Style Come from?

True style comes from within. All the elements and the raw materials of an individual's personality are waiting to be plucked out and turned toward the world. The charismatic person is the one who can identify these certain elements, put them together, and organize them into a unique and winning personality.

There is one definite hurdle you must clear before acquiring style and charisma. You must be on good terms with yourself and know exactly *who* you are and *what* you are, and, conversely, who you are not and what you are not.

Many people—I suggest that the real measure may be "most people"—live their whole lives not knowing who they are or what they are. They have never been able to see the truth about themselves. Why not? Because they have successfully hidden it from themselves.

Indeed, they have unconsciously erected barriers to screen their true selves from the scrutiny of others, and in so doing they have obscured their own self-view. Psychologists recognize that the average person is a mysterious combination of conscious and unconscious motivations that tend to compartmentalize the organism into competing and contradictory boxes.

The problem becomes, then, one of tearing down these barriers, recognizing one's true persona, and concentrating one's separate psychological elements into a personable and glowing entity.

LEARNING HOW TO BE YOU

All growth is a series of trials and errors. As a child you begin to stand and to walk. After many falls, you eventually stay on your own feet and move forward. The same growth pattern occurs in speech. As a child you learn to mouth sounds, and then you learn to control them. The growth pattern is familiar in table manners, in classroom comportment, and in every other learning effort you consciously attempt.

And yet, at the same time you are establishing the learning patterns that make you what you are, you are also going through a series of ages, or changes, that force patterns of behavior on you in your effort to learn to cope not only with things but with other people as well.

For example, you become acutely aware of the rules of behavior laid out so painstakingly by society and enforced by your parents. Even if you find it difficult to obey all these rules, you try. You establish a consciously planned pattern of individual behavior that is yours and that makes you the individual creature that you are.

Consciousness of Self

Other considerations are always present. Your relationships with other members of society frequently cross over to contradict your own rules of behavior, your special ways of obeying those rules. Your relationship with other individuals continually brings about a reexamination of your conduct. Are you shirking the rules? Are you paying too much attention to them?

Emulation of a favored role model may inspire you to change your own lifestyle and behavior patterns. To perfect the persona you want to have, you must become conscious of your self and of your habits. If you pay *too* much attention to your behavior and become obsessed by your ability or inability to portray yourself the way you want to appear, then you become what is called "self-conscious."

The word "conscious" in this sense is a misnomer. Consciousness is not self-knowledge. Self-consciousness is a negative quality, a stumbling block to honesty, to naturalness, and to the revelation of the real you.

Erecting Barriers to True Expression

Almost everyone experiences a certain amount of self-consciousness. It is a part of the human condition. But if you let self-consciousness interfere with your actions, it can neutralize an important positive attribute of your psyche: your self-esteem.

The problem is that your projected image of self may not appear to be materializing correctly. You may be inhibited by social contacts, by personal attributes, and by lack of self-esteem. These obstacles may force your image into a quite different aspect from what you hope it to be. Worse, you may not perceive your true image, through self-deception, through inhibition, or through inability to see yourself clearly.

Clarity of observation is prevented by the barrier of self-consciousness you have erected. The prototype is the person who is not in touch with him- or herself. This person is not wholly integrated into one individual personality, and is, in effect, split up into *two* personalities, the imagined personality and the real personality.

The person out of touch with him- or herself can never be in complete control. No one in such a confused state can be "natural." No one who is a bundle of contradictions can ever hope to project "style." No one who is out of control can ever hope to project "charisma."

The way to get in touch with yourself is, first, through self-analysis, then through a subsequent exercise in retraining and redirecting your psyche, and, finally, through rebuilding of your self into a person more like the one you really want to be.

How can you do it?

First of all, you have to know both your inner and outer self for what you are, and understand yourself without frills, without hopes, without self-deception.

The Man with the Manhattan

A few days ago I had a business appointment with a man whom I had never met in person, but with whom I had conversed briefly on the telephone. We decided to meet for lunch at Le Manoir at the bar.

"How will I know you?" I asked him.

"Oh, I'm in my thirties, I've got a cleft chin like Cary Grant, and I'm about six feet tall, with blue eyes and dark hair. You can't miss me. Besides that, I'll be drinking a Manhattan."

I got to the restaurant and looked around. My man certainly had not yet arrived. There was a group of three at the bar, chatting together. Two singles sat at the near end, engaged in nonverbal communication. A willowy woman with a faraway look sat staring off into space. The only other individual was an enormous rumple of a man with thick horn-rimmed glasses, a hairpiece, a double chin, and a baggy suit.

I hung around, looking out the window into the busy street.

Two People Struggling inside One.   This went on for fifteen minutes. Finally, I got into conversation with the bartender. It turned out that the man on the end was waiting for someone he had never seen before, obviously me. I turned to look at him in astonishment. The rumpled fat man was drinking a Manhattan. *He* was my luncheon date! The glasses? The girth? The hairpiece? Forget it!

I went over and introduced myself.

"I knew you'd recognize me," he said complacently.

I refrained from comment.

Actually, we had an entertaining luncheon. But I've often thought how out of touch with himself that man was, and is. He did not like the fact that he was overweight; he simply ignored it. He did not like the fact that he wore heavy glasses; he ignored that, too. He did not like to admit that he was bald and wearing a rug; he ignored that as well. In his description to me he failed to mention the one facet of his appearance that was the most obvious—he looked like a fat slob.

Even so, he *could* have clued me in a lot more easily by saying something like:

"Oh, I'm taking a crash diet course, but I haven't made any dents in myself yet. I'll be wearing glasses, and I'll be drinking a Manhattan at the end of the bar."

Getting in Touch with Yourself

Drawing a Picture of Yourself.   The first step in getting in touch with yourself is to sit down before a mirror and study yourself as objectively as you can. Unless you are as handsome as Narcissus or as beautiful as Helen of Troy, you will find *something* there that bothers you. If you are normal, there will be a lot there that you do not particularly like.

Lesson 1. You cannot pretend that you do not look like that image in the mirror, because you *do*. Yet you must remember that other people already see you as you *really* are and that they are not negatively affected by your appearance. Since that is surely the case, why should *you* be?

Selecting the Key Feature.   The second step in getting in touch with yourself is to select the feature of your face that you think is best. Hair? Eyes? Nose? Mouth? Shape of face? Masculinity? Femininity?

Probably you have always known your most distinctive feature, and it is quite likely that you already accentuate it in some way to make it the key feature, as you should do.

Lesson 2. Once you have selected your key feature, you must remember to use it as a central reference point in the creation of your image. You should use it to describe yourself to others. By remembering it as your main feature, you can proceed to construct the rest of your persona upon it. And once you have decided on that feature, you must determine how to make it even *more* attractive or arresting. Then you will create an image that is even more individual, even more noticeable, and even more exceptional—and unforgettable!

The Search for the Exceptionable.   Finding the good feature is only part of the process of getting in touch with yourself. The next step is in finding the worst. Hair? Nose? Chin? Mouth? Teeth? Ears?

Everyone has one or two bad features. Even the most beautiful person has a "bad" side. Everyone has moles and warts. Try to put your bad feature, or features, in the proper perspective.

If it happens to be your nose, think of Pinocchio. His nose kept on growing forever. Your nose is not quite so bad as that! Look at yourself again. Admit it. You *could* be in worse shape.

Lesson 3. The ploy is to think of your flaws, to admit them, to realize what they are, but to know they could be worse, and to rise above them. To a degree, ignore them. The thing *not* to do is to pretend that they do not exist. Live with them. That is the law of nature.

Breaking Yourself up into Parts.   Self-knowledge is not the easiest thing in the world to attain. Most people never even try to know themselves. Instead, they fashion themselves into versions of other people and, as a result, become nothing but a bad imitation.

Take an inventory of what you consider to be your strong points of character. I am talking about the elements of your personality that exert the most influence on your actions.

Are you, for example, passive or active? Optimistic or pessimistic? Serious or frivolous? Do you have a sense of humor or do you just *think* you have one? Are you gregarious or shy? Robust or delicate?

Lesson 4. Make up a true inventory and study it carefully. By putting together all the pieces that are you, you should be able to create a picture of yourself as others see you. Keep that picture in mind and carry it about with you so that you know exactly who you are in those crucial first five minutes when you meet someone new.

Criticism and What to Do with It.   Think back to criticisms that have been made of you in the past. Never take all such criticisms seriously; many are shots taken for a specific purpose; many are exaggerated. But you should *think* about them because there may be *something* to them.

Think beyond verbal communication. Study nonverbal statements. People usually volunteer what they really think of you; if you are truly sensitive, you may be able to pick up these thoughts and use them to improve yourself. In this way you will be able to find out what makes you stand out in the eyes of others.

Lesson 5. With all these points in mind and with your own inventory, you can get a good idea of who you are, where you are, and where you are going. From this overall acclimatization you can develop your behavior to emphasize and polish what you like in your nature and at the same time underplay and minimize those things that you do not care for.

Increasing Your Self-confidence

Once you have learned how to be you, there are many different ways you can nourish your own character and in so doing increase your own self-confidence. There are certain pitfalls and certain setbacks you will experience. The following tips on self-confidence may be able to help you through some of the dark days that are sure to come.

- Always have a thorough awareness of and an understanding of your strengths and your weaknesses before you set any goals in your mind. By the time you understand your limitations, you can set yourself certain goals that are within reach and that can be attained. In the long run you will not fail. You will probably stumble along the way to some of the minor goals that you set, but do not blame yourself too much if you do. Do not despair. Let yourself off the guilt hook and try again.
- Do not limit yourself by remembering negative incidents that happened in the distant past. The truth of the matter is that the physical being has no memory of pain. Reversals and bad things that happen are carried in the intellect alone, not in the psyche. Forget the bad. Remember the good.
- In building up a persona, choose the objectives that you value most in your life. Pick out what you really believe in. If you set your goals toward ambitions that you really want to achieve, you will find them easier to attain.
- One thing to understand when you are building up an image is that you are not completely detached from everything in the

universe. You have roots, you have tradition behind you, you have continuity with the past. Past, present, and future—these are all things that are important to the consideration of your goals in life.

- When a setback occurs that tends to undermine your confidence, do not let it throw you, and do not look into your own personality for the answer to the setback. Quite likely the setback occurred because of outside forces. Physical, economic, and political aspects of your life can cause things to go wrong at any time. These are not your fault. If they are uncontrollable, do not try to control them. Work out some way to combat them without changing your goals.

- Never allow yourself to feel guilt or shame over your actions, even though it is sometimes tempting to do so. Many people burden themselves with guilt that is not theirs to bear. You will be slowed down and will waste precious energy in worry and anguish. Unburden yourself of guilt as soon as you recognize its presence. Shame is a personal and individual assessment and should be carefully examined before you allow yourself to be overcome by it.

- Be tolerant of others. People make mistakes. You yourself have made many. As you are tolerant of others, be tolerant of your own actions. There are at least two different ways of looking at every act that takes place. Do not assume that everyone else is out to hurt you.

- Allow your actions to be open to evaluation by others and by yourself as well. What you do should be open to improvement. But do not let other people criticize you as a person. Keep the personal side separate from what you do. Do not criticize anyone else as a person; only criticize *acts* of that person.

- It is easy to get into the habit of putting yourself down. It allows you to feel pity for yourself. You may think others will be nicer to you if they feel sorry for you. That idea is a fallacy. It is not true. A self-pitying attitude is the worst thing you can adopt in order to make people like you.

- If a person, a chore, or a situation becomes intolerable to you, study it carefully. Do not allow it to become a stumbling block to your progress. Pass it by as soon as you can. There are better things in life than meeting every obstacle head-on.

- Be sure to take time off the job to relax, to meditate, and to enjoy hobbies and recreational hours. Quality time is time to get in tune with yourself. You should be able to devote a number of hours every day to your own psyche and your own personality—the most important possessions you have. Do not let them get out of tune. Set aside a certain amount of quality time for this effort.

- Examine carefully each failure and disappointment that occurs in your personal life. Each may be able to give you some clue as to what you are doing wrong. A failure may be the best warning of all to you that your goals are not realistic.

- Be sure to let others know what you want from them. Also let them know what you can do for them in return. Keep reminding others that you are ready to share time with them and take on some of their troubles as well as their joys. Practice being a social animal.

- Keep evaluating your progress as you go along toward your long-range goals. Establish specific, short-range minigoals that are realistic and practical. As you win a small victory, you gain confidence. Be sure your long-range goals are broad enough to allow for alterations you might want to make as you approach them.

- If you experience a deep hurt, simply turn the other cheek. Your ego is not a fragile thing. It is stronger than you yourself. An ego can be hurt, but it can never be demolished or fractured beyond repair. Do not insulate yourself from the world because your ego is bruised. Everyone suffers if you do. The wise person ignores bruises to the ego.

- You always have to be in charge of the direction of your life. Things do not usually come out exactly the way you want them to, but you can hold your goals in sight no matter what happens. When you develop confidence, you will forget all about the "self" in "self-confidence" and become absorbed in living your own life. Then you will be the unique individual who can make the right things happen to you.

THE "TOLERABLE DISTANCE" PHENOMENON

In getting in touch with yourself and maintaining a steady and synchronized persona, you need to find out how effectively you relate to other people. That is, you must discover whether you tend to be warm or cool, or close or distant, in your business relationships.

The key phrase here is "close or distant." In business the concept of "intimacy" is every bit as important as it is in a person's social life outside commercial circles. Intimacy in business circles, however, is somewhat different from intimacy in a family circle.

In a moment I want to discuss some scientific tests that will give you facts and figures by which to measure intimacy; in other words, what goes and what does not go in the business milieu. And there are also ways that you can measure other people's reactions to the amount of intimacy you will be allowed.

But right now I am discussing a simple point: whether you are a hot person or a cool person.

Look back on your own early family life. Childhood is the most intimate time in anyone's history. Every family tends to establish a code of "tolerable distance" between its members. It is within this tolerable distance that you learn how much to touch or not to touch the other, how much to fight or to withdraw, how much to share feelings or to bottle them up.

Note: Distance is crucially important in business dealings of all kinds. A too-aloof attitude and physical presence can be just as damaging as a too-close, too-intimate physical presence. It is mandatory for you to study this phenomenon and find out how to control it in all important job-related situations.

Getting back to your family atmosphere: Try to recollect its feeling. You will discover whether you have a predisposition toward forming emotional bonds that are warm or that are cold. For example, did you hug and kiss your mother? Your father? Your sisters? Your brothers? How much conflict and fighting were allowed in your house? How much distance did you have to maintain between yourself and your family? Did you have "your own space"?

It's Another World Out There

Remember that the business world is quite different from the family world. No one has the same interest in or even understanding of you in the sense that members of your family may have had. If you are used to warm, intimate relationships, you must realize that the people you meet in business are not likely to go in for warm relationships on the spur of the moment. Your own behavior in a business situation should be somewhat near the middle ground between a very warm and a very cold relationship.

Psychologists have established a few basic rules of distances between people to measure this abstract value. There are, in fact, a few rough rules of thumb—in inches and feet—as to how close two people should be and should not be for normal business situations.

Important note: Do not forget that the first five minutes of a business meeting involves a period that is not—repeat, *not!*—an intimate situation. However, there are personality dynamics at work during this crucial period that have a great deal to do with determining *psychological* intimacy, and that can be put to use in making those five minutes important to your success in impressing others with your integrity, business acumen, and overall probity.

THE FOUR RULES OF INTIMACY

Distances people use in communicating with one another can be divided for convenience into four categories, beginning with the least intimate and moving on to the most intimate. Here they are.

1. Lecture distance
2. Business distance
3. Personal distance
4. Intimate distance

1. Lecture Distance

When you are more than twelve feet from another person, you are said to be at "lecture" distance from him or her. This means that there is a minimum of intimacy between you and your companion. It is not quite shouting distance—or "hog-calling range," as they say in the farm belt—but almost. It requires a raised voice, at least, to communicate adequately. This is the farthest distance that by any strength of the imagination can be called "intimate."

2. Business Distance

The second range of distance between people varies from twelve feet to four feet. If that range of distance separates you and your companion, you are considered to be at a "business" distance, or at a typically normal "social" distance. This range is usually reserved for most people in business situations, for store clerks, waiters and waitresses, conversations on the street, and for other casual meetings.

3. Personal Distance

The third range of distance between people measures from four feet to one and a half feet. At this range, you are at what psychologists call a "personal" range. This particular distance is usually reserved for business associates who know one another fairly well, or who are working together on a project, or who are discussing something that sometimes rises above the strictly routine office situation.

4. Intimate Distance

The fourth range of distance between people is at one and a half feet—eighteen inches—or less. This range is reserved for intimate business friends, such as long-time partners, for members of the business family, or for close board-room colleagues. Intimate position is reserved for acquaintances with whom you have been on a business basis for a long time, for most private business confidences, and for members of the opposite sex in whom you are seriously interested.

THE "FOUR SEASONS" OF INTIMACY

Obviously, during the first five minutes of a meeting, you should place yourself at a distance somewhere between four to twelve feet away from your companion. Sitting at a table in a restaurant or sitting behind a desk in an office places you at the proper range for this type of meeting.

However, there are several different stages of business and social intimacy—the type involving people four to twelve feet away—and I would like to examine these stages in greater detail.

I like to think of these stages as "seasons." These seasons do not follow one another in the order of summer, fall, winter, and spring but they do follow one another in situations of varying degrees of coldness and warmth. The following order has to do with increasing business intimacy. You will note that the four seasons of business intimacy actually overlap three of the original categories of distance: partially in the "business" or "social" distance, all of the "personal" distance, and only some of the "intimate" distance (if any at all).

The four seasons are these:

1. The "eye" season
2. The "body" season
3. The "lean" season
4. The "touch" season

1. The "Eye" Season

This is the opener for business dealings between two people. In the clumsy locution of psychology, it is known as "eye contact." Actually, there is no easier way to express the idea. It involves a simple look at someone else. You look directly into the eyes of the person you are addressing or facing. When that person returns your gaze, eye contact is established. This is the key to "eye" intimacy.

2. The "Body" Season

The second step in the establishment of intimacy refers to the orientation of your body toward the body of your companion. It usually involves facing the other person in a one-on-one stance or in a sitting position. When two people are facing one another, this is the ultimate in body posture for intimacy.

3. The "Lean" Season

This is the third step in increasingly businesslike intimacy. The eyes have met, the bodies have arranged themselves so that they face one another for maximum viewing and assessing. Now you want to establish more intimacy. You lean forward, usually at the hips, with the top of the body moving your head closer to your companion's. Not *too* close. That may come later.

4. The "Touch" Season

This is the fourth step in business meetings between two people. It is the final closing of the circuit of intimacy. When you touch the other person with your hand so that you can feel their skin, business intimacy has been completed and trust has been established. The handshake is the ultimate seal of confidence and assurance. It is the seal of approval on a business deal.

MAKING THE MOST OF THE EYES

Although the eyes are only part of your total facial makeup, they are extremely important as part of body language. When you look directly into someone else's eyes, you are engaging in one of the most important elements of communication. Eye contact is equal in force to the sound of the voice and its tone.

Even more expression can be produced by eye contact than by voice contact. It is through the eyes that you become involved with another person on a search-and-analyze basis; it is one of the most intimate exchanges outside actual physical touch.

Because eye contact is so powerful and effective in business, as anywhere else, you can use it to draw someone to you, physically or psychologically, or at least you can cause someone else to look more closely at you to see why you are interested.

Rule: Eye contact is *not* to be used to disturb. Never be a starer, the equivalent of the "breather" on the other end of the telephone line. Use eye contact to establish sincerity, not to upset your business contact. When you look directly in the eyes of another person, you generally give that person the idea that you are telling the truth. Do not risk ruining that precept by turning your look into a dull stare.

MAKING THE MOST OF THE BODY

The placement of the body is most important when you meet another person. If you place your body head-on with someone else, you can mean one of two things:

1. You can mean that you are defenseless and therefore are in a disarmed position for honest, "trust-me," give-and-take.
2. You can mean that you are facing directly someone you consider to be an opposing force. Then you are in direct opposition to a predetermined opponent.

This brings me to my first rule of body placement.

Rule 1. Never place your body head-on with a stranger. It is better to turn the body slightly to one side, or to face a person indirectly, so as to reduce the pressure that is automatically created by the posture of confrontation.

A little reconnaissance is in order here. The next time you are walking down the street, watch people who meet one another or stop to chat. You will notice that as they become more friendly and animated and are no longer strangers, their orientation tends to become more head-on, more direct, and more relaxed.

What can be considered confrontation without the proper warming up by both parties can actually become the precursor of intimacy if you handle the situation with the proper body orientation.

Making the Most of the Torso

The simple and effortless movement of leaning forward during a business conversation can increase intimacy without overstepping the bounds of propriety. You can use body language in this manner to tell someone else that you are warming up to him or her. You can also use it to show considered aggression, to express possible opposition, or to warn against unconscious appropriation.

The best way to use this subtle kind of body language in a business conversation is to await the proper moment in the dialogue and use it to respond to something the other person has said. Your movement then underlines the fact that you are in complete accord with the thoughts expressed.

It is best to study your business associate at all times during your speech in order to ascertain if he or she is responding and wants to be reacted to in this fashion. Many people simply do not want closer intimacy at *any* time.

And that brings me to the second rule of body placement.

Rule 2. In using body language, you must become adept in reading what others think of you in their own body language. If you respond incorrectly because you have read their signals inaccurately, you can blow the whole deal you are trying to set up.

When strangers in business become friends and the relationship prospers and becomes something more than formal, then you can use the act of leaning forward in a manner that is more than a simple expression of accord. You can actually tell your business associate that a more intimate relationship has been established, based on trust and confidence.

But wait for the proper moment. Timing is essential in this most crucial statement of intimacy.

Making the Most of Touching

Touching is the most aggressive and personal body movement you can make. Most people will be repulsed by the touch of your hand in an intimate gesture during your first five minutes of meeting them. Between two males, touching may be interpreted incorrectly. Among females, touching does not have such negative connotations. Nevertheless, it should be carefully considered.

And that brings me to the third rule of body placement.

Rule 3. Touching should be avoided during the early moments of a business conversation between two people. Many do not use it at all—ever. You must try to judge whether or not to use it by watching the other person's reactions to such an approach. Do not try it too soon, no matter how warm the signals may seem. Kissing is a Hollywood habit as meaningless as the wave of a hand; it is not appropriate in the ordinary business situation.

During the first five minutes of a meeting, intimacy is out. And yet you can use all the other steps leading up to actual touch—the handshake—in those first five minutes, if any *one* of them seems appropriate. I stress the word "one" and want to explain why.

One "Season" at a Time, Please

It is never right to employ more than one of the four "seasons"— eye, body, lean, or touch—at one time, especially during any first meeting.

Eye contact is the least overpowering, but it should not be overdone.

Once you have established eye contact, you can then turn your body toward your companion, and keep it turned.

After a little bit, you may even lean toward your companion, but do not do it overtly or obviously. Let it happen.

As for touch, watch it carefully. Never combine it with any other of the signs of intimacy, except in a guarded way with eye contact.

And that brings me to my fourth rule of body placement, which is as follows:

Rule 4. This is the simplest rule of all. Do not combine any of the four "seasons" of intimacy during a first meeting. Use only one at a time, and use it charily.

It is best to use eye contact as a two-edged blade. Use it to inform the other person that you are establishing a bond between the two of you; use it at the same time to study what the other person is doing as you converse. If you find that eye contact is distasteful—for example, if your companion shies away from it—do not persist, but glance to the side or look at a potted palm or another diner to take the pressure off.

If your companion deliberately moves away from you when you lean forward, avoid such a move until you are sure it will not cause discomfort or embarrassment. When in doubt, avoid leaning close.

The same applies to body position. Try out the various positions. The one that is the most comfortable, that causes you the least nervousness and tension—provided it does not bother your companion—is the proper one to maintain.

It is mostly a matter of testing.

CONVERSATION WITHOUT WORDS

It is always a good idea to be completely aware of the nonverbal signals being given off by the person to whom you are speaking. Study the body language and the facial expressions to see how your act is going over. Then also study your companion's voice, its pitch, and listen to the words.

From these reactions you can assess whether or not you are establishing good or bad vibrations between the two of you. These considerations are much more important than the actual words being spoken in the conversation.

The Truth About Intimacy

As you can see when you study someone you do not know at all, it is the threat of intimacy that for some reason unnerves most people who are in contact with you, even in a business situation where no idea of sex obtrudes. This fear of intimacy is a false fear at best.

Touch, warmth, contact—these are simple and nonthreatening things. If you look at them and analyze them carefully, you will find that they are simply elements of closeness, and closeness does not demand immediate fireworks and sexual ecstasy. A light slap on the back of a friend and a grip of the elbow or shoulder does not immediately presage a session in bed.

Intimacy is really a ritual of friendship that occurs frequently in a board room or a kitchen. It is a simple fact of life; animals experience intimacy exactly as human beings do. Animals are not always coupling; nor are human beings.

TALKING STRAIGHT OUT

In business you must be able to talk straight to other people. This is not an easy thing to do. From your first hours on earth you hide your feelings behind a mask of politeness and conceal your private thoughts from others. You have dozens of masks, façades, and faces that become mixed up with your true face. Business intimacy means that you must subject yourself to a certain risk of vulnerability.

You must, for example, take off all the masks and risk being seen naked among your business intimates. There can never be closeness without honesty. You must practice clear speech—I mean speech that is not hiding anything—in order to make your real feelings known. You must be able to tell what pleases *and* what displeases.

FACING YOUR SEPARATENESS

You *are* an island, as well as a part of the whole, as much as John Donne would like you not to believe it. Each individual is separate and apart from everyone else. To be human means to accept the problem of being independent from others. This means that you have to decide on what to do with your life, who your friends will be, and how you will deal with setbacks and with triumphs in your business dealings. Your burden is the burden of freedom, something that we cherish in this country without really accepting it for what it is. I am talking about the awesome responsibility for being in control of your own life.

Because you are an island, you must take your time in developing any kind of relationship with another island. That kind of relationship, even in a business sense, is an intimate one. Intimacy can never be instantaneous like certain packaged foods.

It develops at its own pace, usually slowly and surely. There may be business ventures that start up quickly, but these, like evanescent love affairs, sometimes extinguish themselves overnight. Intimate business ventures that count are usually slow in developing and solid enough to withstand all the assaults of circumstances and the crises of life.

Remember this every time you meet someone for business purposes. It will put in proper perspective the extreme importance of those initial moments together, when you decide to go ahead with your new contact . . . or not.

That is what getting down to business in those first five minutes is really all about.

7

THE JOB INTERVIEW: MINUTE BY MINUTE

Nowhere in the business world are the first five minutes more important than in the job interview. Those five minutes can be the most important time of your life. It may be the misstep that commits you to a series of failures that are almost impossible to overcome; or it may be that important step up that portends overall success for the rest of your life.

There is one primary rule to remember, and I advise you to type that primary rule out on a three-by-five filing card and slip it into the side of the bathroom mirror so that you can see it every morning.

That rule is divided into three parts:

1. Sell yourself.
2. Sell your skill.
3. Sell your potential.

The first part of the rule is the most important, and I will talk about it first. Not only is selling *yourself* more important than selling your *skill* or your *potential,* but you must sell it first, before proceeding to work on the other parts.

THE BIG JOB INTERVIEW

I know a young writer who was convinced that he would become the Great American Novelist. He was writing stories all through high school and all through college. During his collegiate years he got his big chance. Through a short-story contest at the university he was able to place as one of the top three candidates for a job in the writing department of a major motion-picture studio.

His stories were certainly acceptable in the eyes of the university faculty committee that had selected them and him as winning items. They were good enough to get him an interview at the studio. His potential was obvious, as was his skill.

But take a look at what happened.

Rick recently looked back on that interview and told me how it went for use in this book in the job-interview chapter.

Rick's Story in His Own Words

I was full of beans about that interview [Rick told me]. I knew this would be my ticket to the big time. I wasn't one of those dilettantes, one of those people who looks on writing as being inspired by the gods before a word is put down on paper. I was a working writer, and I turned out reams of copy. Most of it was good. Certainly it was dramatically workable, and after all, this was the movie business.

I had never worked for anyone at the time of the interview. You know, on a paying basis. I had the idea that what you did meant more than who you were. That was part of my upbringing, probably, and part of my exposure to the mores of business and entertainment through the narrow tunnel-vision confines of the university system.

At the start of the interview I was ushered into this office with three middle-aged gentlemen seated in chairs around a desk. These were very well-dressed people in expensive tweed jackets and slacks and ties—all three of them—and I saw them looking over my manuscripts.

So I sat there while they pawed through them. Finally one of them—he seemed to be the head guy—glanced up and said:

"You like to write?"

I leaned back and smiled. "Of course I like to write! I'm not one of those people who has to be *inspired* to write."

He nodded as if assimilating my comment. Then he touched one of the manuscripts. "These won't play, you know."

I was startled. "They're not meant to be screenplays."

He smiled. "I suppose not. They're terribly derivative."

Certainly they were derivative. "Isn't everything? Isn't Shakespeare?"

"But *his* played," said the Chief Prosecutor.

The second guy broke in. "It bothers me that you like to write. I always considered writing a damned hard thing to do. And yet you *like* it."

"I never said it was easy. I said I *liked* it."

The second guy shrugged. Then the first came back on.

"You can't get away with parody here. There's not an original thought in these stories."

I thought about all the movies I'd been seeing in the past few years. Not one of them had an original idea, either. But if I said that . . .

"Look," said the third guy. "We like this stuff. It's fun to read. But I don't know what we can do with it."

I sat there wondering what to say. The first guy finally stood up. "It's been a pleasure talking to you. We'll let you know."

Needless to say, I didn't get the chance to work as a story-department apprentice.

Rick had neglected the first and most important point in any job interview. He had not bothered to sell himself. He had thought his product was more important than his persona.

An analysis of Rick's story about his job interview points up several important points about *any* job interview. The interviewers were using Rick's stories as a typical interviewer will use a résumé. Rick's stories were his résumé, really. The stories were examples of his previous experience.

The potential was there, but potential is the third most important part of any job interview, as I pointed out at the beginning of the chapter. The second most important point—skill or commodity—was not really there in those stories, either. The interviewers were not holding possible scripts in their hands, as Rick well knew. They were trying to work out what Rick himself was like. It was his persona that was up for sale, not his stories or his creativity.

Rick, like many other people in a first interview, had missed the point of the meeting.

Later on, looking back on that interview, Rick could see what he had done wrong. He wrote it down for me.

Rick's Analysis in His Own Words

If I had that interview to do over, I'd pitch it in an entirely different way. I'd pitch *myself*, my gut instincts about writing, my desire to tell stories.

You see, I had missed the point in the interviewer's first question. He was giving me a chance to tell him *why* I wanted to write, not simply to brag about being a doer and not a dreamer. Hell, he knew I wasn't a dreamer. I had already written stories, hadn't I? He had them in his hand.

I should have answered him something like this:

"I hate to write. But I like to capture what makes people tick in story form—to get it down on paper for others to read."

Then the interviewer could have proceeded along another line. He could have asked me if I thought I was able to write stories in screenplay form. Obviously I could, but I had to learn how to.

That was the point of the interview. They were there to teach me screen-writing techniques. Had I answered in that fashion, then they would have ticked one up for me. They would have seen I wanted to learn, that I was potential clay for their molding.

I missed the point.

Also, when one of them accused me of writing derivative material, I should have come back with: "The great writers use derivative material. The trick is to flesh out what's derivative and make it into something new and bigger."

Those guys weren't fools. They knew movies were derivative. So what? But they backed me into a corner. I thought I'd be insulting them if I said their stuff was derivative too.

Actually, the ploy wasn't to counterattack, the ploy was to use that idea as a steppingstone to another: creative derivation.

I had the ideas, I had the knack, I had the partial skills. But, damn it, I failed to let them see that I had the skills *and* the desire.

I sat there not realizing what a jerk I was!

Rick was not a jerk. Rick was simply not thinking enough at that point to realize that he was not being interviewed for his written material, but for himself, for the writer inside him, for the psyche that would eventually be harnessed to dream up motion-picture scripts for the studio.

A point to remember: At a job interview, you are selling yourself first and foremost. Only when you have succeeded in selling yourself can you go on to peddle your skills and your potential. *Never forget this basic point of the job interview.*

WHY MANY INTERVIEWS FAIL

Although it is never advisable to accentuate the negative, I would like to switch the signals for a moment and explore negatives. It is in a good cause.

There are six main reasons that people flunk interviews for high-level positions below the chief-executive-officer level. One recruiting firm has isolated these six from the records of more than two hundred failed candidates. Here are the Big Bad Six.

1. Poor appearance, dress, and/or grooming
2. Inability to express views clearly
3. Failure to project self objectively
4. Incompetence in projecting self-confidence and enthusiasm
5. Overcriticism of former employers
6. Too much evidence of job jumping

You will note that the first four reasons are related to shortcomings of the persona and that all four have been analyzed in this book already. The last two have to do with career-oriented problems.

GETTING READY FOR THE INTERVIEW

The best way to decide what to wear to a job interview is to try to dress in conformity with the codes of the employees in the office where the interview is held. If you cannot investigate before the meeting, simply take a sample of the dress around your own office. If you have been in the work force for awhile, you will be pretty much aware of what is allowed and what is not. If you have been out of it for awhile, or have never been in it, visit a few offices where friends work and take a look around.

Special note: If you are new to the work force and are interviewing for your first job, read the next section carefully. If you are not, skip it and go on to the one following.

Announcing Your Commitment

Dress codes in offices change with the times. Jeans and shirttails were fine for a few years, but in some corporate sites you cannot get away with that kind of image anymore. In fact, you must look around and think about your clothes today much more than in the recent past.

As it happened, just as I was preparing this manuscript for the printer, a story appeared in the newspaper about university graduates suiting up for job interviews. What it all boiled down to was what one young man said:

> I don't think you could get a job with a tie, but I'm sure you could lose a job with the *wrong* tie.

Right on!

In the story women graduates were doing the same act. Said one who had purchased a dark suit with several accessories such as silk blouses and rep ties:

> It's as if you're buying a uniform.

Another woman graduate stated for the interviewer:

> My gray pinstriped suit is the most boring piece of clothing I ever wore. I am announcing my commitment to the world of banking. I want to create an image that will make them focus on me *as a person* rather than on me as an incorrect dresser.

Analyzing that remark further, the article noted that the woman who had committed herself to the world of banking by wearing a gray pinstriped suit had originally worn a skirt and sweater to her first interview. And that, of course, was a mistake she would not make again. About that gaffe, she commented:

> I stuck out like a sore thumb!

There is a happy ending to her story. Next day she bought the gray suit.

From the standpoint of the job interviewers, however, all that worry seemed a little bit like overkill. One of them was quoted as saying:

We expect prospects to be tidy and to wear suits or nice dresses, but they should look like students, rather than executives. After all, we don't expect them to look as they would if they *worked* here. They're not corporate types—yet.

I would like you to note that word "yet." A word to the wise . . .

One final word: No matter what your status, decide what you want to wear to a job interview several days in advance. Then you will not find yourself fuming and fretting and wearing yourself out on the big day if you have a button off or a rip in a seam.

GETTING TO THE INTERVIEW ON TIME

Be sure to arrive at the interview site at least fifteen minutes ahead of time. If you come in late, you are going to get bad marks. Lateness makes a negative impression. Not only does it show that you cannot be trusted, but it makes you a nervous wreck to boot. When you are flustered and apologetic, instead of calm and self-contained, you do not come off as well as you would ordinarily.

If the company is a big one, let yourself have enough time to find the proper office where the interview is to be held.

When you get to the receptionist, be sure to check for the proper pronunciation of the interviewer's name. While you sit there waiting, think of an opening line for the interview. You should have a number of different openings in mind so that you can select the most appropriate when you are finally on the scene.

If the receptionist seems amicable, you can always begin a low-key conversation. Small talk is best. Sometimes you will receive clues about the company or even about the interviewer.

The First Minute

Your entrance into the interviewer's office can make or break your entire meeting. Walk in with your head up, your back straight, your face smiling, your attitude energetic and animated.

The best impression to make at this crucial point is that of someone pleasant and interesting. The first impression you make is *crucial*. You will never get a chance to make it again.

Once you are inside the office, look the interviewer straight in the eye and shake hands firmly. Then, if the interviewer does not intervene and tell you where to sit, go for the upright chair. It is easier to look alert straight up in a hardbacked chair than it is sunken down into a puffy couch. If there is no upright chair, sit on the overstuffed couch in an upright position, with only the lower part of your spine touching the back. In other words, do not slump but maintain an erect posture even if you *do* feel comfortable.

Remain eye to eye with the interviewer as much of the time as you can. Do not fidget, pull your hair, swing your legs, or indulge in any other body-language tics.

The Second Minute

Once the meeting is consolidated and the initial inspection on both sides is completed, you must remember that your main purpose in coming to speak to the interviewer is to impress him or her with your own persona in the most favorable way possible. You are not there to sell your past experience or your skills or your expertise. It is a mistake to do so, as I pointed out in the initial anecdote of this chapter. Yet it is a mistake countless people make *every day* in trying out for a job.

Nevertheless, it is important for you to be able to tell the interviewer, if the question comes up, what your skills are and how you have used them in the past. Most of these points will be covered in your résumé anyway. It never hurts to bring them out, if you are asked.

The Third Minute

By now you and the interviewer will have established some kind of rapport. By now, if you are perceptive, you may be able to spot either resistance or acceptance on the part of the interviewer. On the other hand, things may be running smoothly with no indication of how the interviewer feels about you. It really matters very little. You must not allow yourself to relax if you think you *are* making a good impression; at least, it is a bad idea to relax to the extent of lounging in your chair or beginning to appear indolent or amused. Keep your good posture and continue to exert energetic intensity of manner.

The interviewer will probably give you a rundown of the job by describing it at this point in the meeting. Do not assume that this is time for a coffee break and slump down and lose interest. Respond continually to the points being made. They are being made for a reason. It is important for you to react to anything said here.

As the interviewer outlines the job, pay particular attention not only to the words spoken but the *attitude* of the interviewer. You should be reading him or her, just as he or she is reading you.

The Fourth Minute

The interviewer may well give you a chance to talk about yourself. Be selective about what you reveal. Consider the interviewer individually. What might he or she want to discuss with you? You can load up this part of the interview with personal points if you like.

In this fourth minute quite possibly the tension you have felt at first—both you and the interviewer—may have dissipated somewhat. By now the interviewer is making a decision. Is it yes, or no? You will never find out from watching, although you may be getting some good hints by the vibrations in the air.

The best thing is simply to go on and complete the interview without paying attention to what the interviewer is thinking, even if you believe you know.

The Fifth Minute

Questions may begin at this point, questions that have a great deal of relevancy to the situation at hand. Because questions are so important in an interview, particularly the manner in which they are handled, I have compiled a list of possible questions that an interviewer might ask so that you can study them beforehand.

The main thing is not to let any question throw you for a loop. A lot of interviewers like to rattle an interviewee. Actually, if you are up for a job, you are fair game for the person who is looking you over for the position. Any interviewer wants to know how a prospective employee is going to react under stress.

You must expect to get a curve ball thrown once in a while—or maybe even a bean ball.

Five Minutes Plus

Most interviews last longer than five minutes, but the crucial moments will have passed in this time. By now you simply face the questions in your own way and ask questions if you are invited to do so.

One thing you must remember about the job interview: Don't talk too much!

I know one good friend who was trying for a high-level job in marketing. He was a salesperson through and through, and he should have understood the trick of selling himself.

However, he had a very bad habit of overdoing it. In the first fifteen minutes of an interview, he would sell himself completely. And in the last fifteen minutes, he would completely unsell himself.

I have known several interviewers who said the same thing about him.

My advice to you is:

Know when to put a clamp on your tongue.

THE POWER OF POSITIVITY

Your role throughout a job interview is to keep your poise and present all the positive factors in your favor clearly and fully. You will also have to handle all questions that arise and neutralize objections as well as you can.

Remember that no matter how long the interview continues, you may not know at the end of it whether or not you have made the grade and been selected. Usually you have a great deal of competition for the job. Your interviewer may be seeing more people after you; he or she may have seen many before you.

In addition to that, you may be called back for a second interview, even a third in some cases. During these subsequent meetings, there will be a lot more detailed questions you are required to answer. Sometimes there is a considerable amount of discussion before you are hired or not hired.

Through it all remember one most important thing:

Keep your poise!

QUESTIONS, QUESTIONS, QUESTIONS

When you face an interviewer during a job hunt, it is a good idea to know in a general way what you are going to be asked. If you come prepared for the right kind of questions, you stand little chance of being thrown a curve ball by a clever interviewer.

Most interview questions fall into three or four general categories:

1. Work experience
2. Education
3. Family and early years
4. Current activities and interests

Most of your work experience will be listed in your résumé, which the interviewer already has on hand. Be sure, incidentally, to take a copy of your résumé with you, just in case. Many interviewers like to probe beneath the surface facts that are revealed there so briefly. And there may be a good reason for such probing.

Subjects That May Come Up

Here are some possible questions you may be asked, along with some possible answers that may help you to see a way out for yourself in a comparable situation.

Q. **What are your career goals?**
A. "Goals" are very big items these days in hiring halls. Sometimes the question about goals is intended to be a catch ques-

tion, but usually it is a straightforward one. When you answer, be sure that you do not give the impression that you are using the job as a stepping stone to something bigger and—perish the thought!—more important.

Q. Why did you leave your last job?

A. When you answer this question, do not let any bitterness about a former employer show through. It is very easy to put down a former boss, but your prospective employer may hear a note of warning to himself or herself in your response. Just answer the question as honestly and as objectively as you can.

Q. Why does this job interest you?

A. You will have to think this one out and adapt it to your own particular situation. Do not try to be clever or flip. Give an honest answer, even if it might seem a bit obvious. The question is sometimes used as an initiator simply to get you talking.

Q. What do you consider your strengths? Your weaknesses?

A. This is a question you can adapt to the job situation as it exists. Stress what will make the job go well. Make your weaknesses into strengths. That is, stress your perfectionism as a weakness, but let it be accepted as a strength.

Education will be listed on your résumé. If you are applying for your first job, you may be asked about your best and worst subjects in school, how you liked the college atmosphere, if you expanded your activities into extracurricular work of any kind, how you financed your education, what your feelings are regarding authority, leadership, and knowledge.

Some interviewers will be interested in your family and early years, especially if you are trying out for your first job. The point of a question in this general area is to find out how much responsibility you have shouldered and how well you have managed it.

For example, a question about your home life and how you grew up may not be small talk at all. The interviewer may be trying to find out if your early life was stable or may be trying to ascertain how you looked at yourself over the years. A question about your early life may also lead to some kind of information about your degree of motivation and personal adjustment.

Most interviewers include questions about present activities and interests because the answers sometimes give clues about your hobbies and what you do with your spare time. If your hobbies are frivolous, that means something; if they are strange, but have a reason, that means something else. In fact, most employers look for people who are engaged in outside political, volunteer, or professional activities. Prepare yourself accordingly.

Danger: Special Questions

There are some questions that you can refuse to answer if you like. Laws have been passed prohibiting interviewers from asking women applicants any questions about their marital status, their family planning, and the like.

If you do choose to answer a question in this area, simply make a straightforward statement about it.

Interviewers cannot ask anyone about religious or ethnic backgrounds, either. Nor can they ask about specific age.

The problem of money is always a touchy one. When the interviewer asks you how much you are making, quite probably an exaggeration is expected. Most personnel consultants recommend a bit of exaggeration.

Actually, it is very hard for anyone to find out how much money you are really making. No personnel department releases salary information.

Nevertheless it is important for you to know the top number in the salary range of the position for which you are applying.

Some Questions You Might Be Asked

Following are some typical questions that any job interviewer might ask you during a meeting. If you have some kind of answer in mind, you won't have to hem and haw as you try to think up a quick response.

What do you consider to be the most important qualities for filling this job?

———

What do you think will make the difference between success and failure in this job?

——

What is the greatest accomplishment you have ever achieved in your life?

——

What is the greatest failure you have ever experienced in your life?

——

In your last job, was there anything you would rather have done *more* of?

——

If you had the opportunity to give advice to management on your last job, what would it have been?

——

Describe the best boss you ever had.

——

Describe the worst boss you ever had.

——

How do you see your future in this company?

——

In comparison to other jobs you are interviewing for, how does this job rank? Better? Worse? Same?

——

Have you done anything in the past year to improve yourself?

——

What are your greatest strengths?

——

What are your greatest weaknesses?

———

What kind of a boss was your last immediate superior?

———

For what shortcomings do people most often criticize you?

———

What aspects of your last job did you like *least*?

———

What aspects of your last job did you like *best*?

———

What factors in your life have handicapped you and prevented your progress?

———

What factors in your life have helped the most to develop you?

———

If you had your life to live over again, would you do things differently? How?

———

If you were not you, who would you rather be?

———

What minor irritants upset you the most?

———

How does your spouse (if you have one) feel about this job?

———

What do you think management could do to assist you in functioning effectively?

———

What did you do in your spare time last week?

———

What is the hardest thing you have ever done in your life?

———

Are there any of your qualifications that we have not discussed?

———

Is there anything else that you would like to tell me about yourself?

WHAT IS SEEN IS WHAT IS HIRED

One thing I mentioned at the opening of this chapter was the three-part job interview rule, the third part of which reads: Sell your potential.

You cannot step out of your role as a job applicant to point out verbally that your interviewer will be getting a tremendous potential in you if he or she hires you, but you can try to give evidence of the fact in your attitude and in your answers to his or her questions.

What your interviewer sees is what he or she hires or does not hire. Perhaps the interviewer, too, hopes that you will rise above your present level. However, it is a good idea to remind the interviewer of the fact that you are not always going to be as you are *at the moment:* You are going to be better!

The way to point your interviewer into the future is not to tell him or her that you are going to rise level by level in the company until you take over the top job—that smacks too much of Horatio Alger—but that you are quite interested in the potentialities of the company and want to grow along with it.

Although this may strike you as a bit of excessive stroking, it can be effective if stated in a sincere and responsible fashion.

Of course, if the interviewer is afraid you might be better than he or she is, and if you are a bit overqualified for the job you are seeking, this particular ploy may well backfire on you. But that is a chance you have to take.

8

THE SALES INTERVIEW: MINUTE BY MINUTE

When you are face to face with a sales prospect, it all comes together. You immediately find out if your training and spade work will pay off. All those months of getting your act together can come to nothing if you have failed to do your preliminary homework correctly. But if you have done it, then you realize its importance at that time of those first five minutes.

This is the time the sale is made, not the second five minutes or the last handshake.

Each meeting between a salesperson and a prospect is a once-in-a-lifetime thing. Each interaction between pitchperson and potential buyer is an individual one-on-one relationship that can never be repeated. The techniques of selling are as old as the hills, but each particular interview is always brand new. Even though the same kinds of motivations exist on both sides of the desk, even though the same techniques of persuasion are used time after time, and even though the same words crop up year after year—every new sales interview is fresh and special.

THE GAMESMANSHIP OF SELLING

There is a great deal of gamesmanship in selling, a lot of fun in playing the game to win. The best people in the business treat it the way a sportsperson treats a football game, a lawyer treats a trial, or a grocer treats a buyer of fresh vegetables.

Here you are, primed to take on a brand-new client, a client who may turn out to be a feather in your cap with a sale, or to strike out without the consummation of a sale. Which is it going to be?

Although the first five minutes begin to tick off the moment you face your prospect, you must *prepare* for those five minutes a long time beforehand.

In actuality, the first five minutes begins the moment you alight from the cab that carries you to your client's address, the moment you drive into the parking lot of his or her company, or the moment you walk into the building from the busy street.

PREPARING FOR YOUR BIG SCENE

You should be on your best mettle from the moment you come into sight of the prospect's office. There are more people involved in a causal interview than just the two of you. There is the parking-lot attendant who watches you get out of your car in the lot. There is the receptionist who watches you come down the hallway to announce your name. There is the secretary who works for the man or woman you are going to see.

Your appearance makes a lasting impression on all these spear-bearers. You cannot count on slouching wearily into a seat outside the office, sagging with eyelids at half-mast until you are ushered into the office, and then perking up the instant you enter with your sudden best foot forward.

GETTING YOURSELF UP FOR THE PROSPECT

You have to be up the moment you get out of that car, or alight from that cab. The people who surround your target may seem to be only minions to you, but every one of them may be important to your future. The parking attendant may get a negative impression of you if your car is dented, dirty, or sending off waves of black smoke and pollution into the air.

In his or her small office, even the receptionist may be an integral part of the business team you are trying to impress. That person's reaction to your demeanor may make or break the sale.

"I'm Bob Jones. I'm here to see Dick Trent," you say.

Quite probably the receptionist will use the intercom to check on your prospect and will tell you to sit down and wait. Even though your appointment is for the exact moment you have arrived, you probably will not be asked in immediately. There are many reasons for this. Most executives simply have a habit of letting salespersons wait awhile before letting them in.

A TIME OF AWARENESS

Cooling your heels in a reception area can be a lot of dead time on your hands, if you consider it such. But you can use that time to increase your awareness of the company, if you like, and help the people in the company increase their awareness of you. If the receptionist shows any inclination to make conversation, use that loophole to break the ice. However there are two warnings:

1. If the receptionist is busy doing some kind of assignment, or is in desperate disorder trying to take care of a busy switchboard, leave him or her alone. To try to make conversation can only ring down the curtain on you.
2. If the receptionist is of the opposite sex, be very careful not to mix business matters with social matters. Especially for a man, the sleaziest of all images is that of the traveling salesman trying to butter up the secretary to make a big sale. Today, that kind of approach will be greeted—and rightly so!—by some snarling comment about a "male chauvinist."

You can use any kind of icebreaker you wish in order to communicate with the receptionist who seems willing to talk. You can comment on the weather, talk about sports, discuss motion pictures or cable television, new VCRs, books, art, music, or anything that happens to strike your fancy.

BE INTERESTED IN PEOPLE

Consider this kind of communication as simple social interaction and not something inevitably intricate that will lead to *something big*. Small talk about the company itself, or business, or even the neighborhood usually brings out facts that you may be able to use in your sales pitch.

"I haven't seen you here before. Have you been working here long?"

Most people like to talk about their jobs. You can learn a great deal about a company from casual talk with its employees. Sometimes information gathered in this preliminary stage can be of great value to you later on.

You should try to learn the receptionist's name for later use. Be sure you ask it in a fashion that does not signal some kind of clumsy pass; the more subtle the better.

Once you are summoned to your prospect, excuse yourself and go as politely as you can, breaking off the conversation with the comment that you have enjoyed talking and will continue the discussion later on.

THE THIN DANGER LINE

You will then be guided in to see your prospect by his or her assistant or secretary. Here again, try to be as natural and as affable as you can without seeming to be too forward or pushy. Chat with your guide about whatever pops into your mind. Perhaps you have met already on the telephone when you were setting up the appointment. It is a good idea to remember that if the assistant takes a dislike to you, your sale may be in danger of cardiac arrest and you may be in danger of occupying the reject file.

There is a thin line of danger separating too pushy behavior and too unfeeling behavior. To come on with a macho assertiveness (or the opposite, if that applies) is to jeopardize your future relationship with your prospect. To ignore members of the staff and to treat them like pieces of furniture can be just as bad as groping them in a proprietary way.

The right approach is to consider your prospect as your number one target, but not to ignore people who work in supportive positions near him or her. The right approach is to take a friendly attitude, chat about the weather or about working conditions or about personal details if you know them, and let it go at that.

GETTING OFF ON THE RIGHT FOOT

Bear in mind that someone who is an assistant today may be an associate tomorrow and may be more than an associate the day after tomorrow. It is essential that you get off on the right foot with everyone you come in contact with. You never know what is going to happen tomorrow in the great reshuffling of executive titles.

All this preliminary communication is actually preparation for your most important "first five minutes." No matter how well you carry out your first five minutes, however, if your groundwork is not correct you may quite easily sabotage a perfect meeting with your prospect.

The First Minute

Of the first five minutes, the initial sixty seconds that pass are probably the most important of all. It is during this sixty seconds that your prospect's eye sees you as a person, sizes you up as an individual, and watches you as you enter his or her controlled environment.

All the advantage is on the side of the prospect. This is his or her turf. The prospect is completely familiar with it. Actually, he or she invented it. All aids and accessories are close at hand. The prospect feels at home here because, in effect, it is a second home. He or she is welcoming you as a guest, but it is to the *prospect*'s castle, the *prospect*'s terrain.

But the prospect is playing a waiting game. It is up to you to make all the early moves. It is your job to develop his or her interest in what you are going to be talking about. It is you who will get the ball rolling.

The First Move You Make. The first move you make is your entrance. I use the term "entrance" advisedly. The moment you appear in the prospect's office can be appropriately compared to the entrance of an actor or actress on a theater stage. The eyes of the audience, in this case, the eyes of the prospect, are on your every move; the ears of the audience are attuned to what you will say. All attention is focused on you. It is your moment to make or break.

The first impression must be focused entirely on your bodily movements, the expression on your face, the total image that you convey. Although that impression may be supplemented with verbal projections, for the moment I want to analyze the moves you make.

Body Language You Can Use.   Your whole demeanor should convey an impression of friendliness, relaxed confidence, warmth, brightness, and a feeling of total command. To put it into sports terms, you should convey an image of being "up" to the coming interview. You are projecting in your persona, your total self that others trust, respect, and believe in.

The most important element of your total body language is your face. Your face must be relaxed, projecting an impression of confidence and pleasure. You are pleased to meet the prospect. You know that you will get along well with one another. You have something to speak to him or her about. That is all there is to it.

Warning! Watch that eye contact. The most important element of your facial expression is your eyes. Although your mouth and facial muscles are important in conveying a feeling of pleasure, it is the eyes that really do the trick. Your eyes show exactly where your interest is focused. It is surprising to realize how many people do not understand the importance of the eyes. Competitors know the value of watching the eyes: a boxer can tell sometimes when an opponent is going to punch by the flicker of the eye; a football player can tell by the eyes of the quarterback where he is going to throw the ball.

You are eyeing the prospect at the same time the prospect is eyeing you. If, however, you do not eye the prospect and are instead looking around the room at the furniture, the prospect must necessarily deduce that you are not interested in him or her but only in what he or she possesses.

Because of the importance of eye contact, the first rule in meeting someone is to look the person in the eye and maintain that eye contact all through the interview. This advice is old-fashioned, but it is important.

Watch it! I am not talking about a staring contest in which you try to break the eyeballs of your opponent. That kind of contest becomes an adversary relationship, the thing you certainly want to avoid at all costs. Certainly you should drop your eyes away from his or her eyes every so often. But make it clear that the prospect's eyes are your particular target all during the interview. Looking away, commenting on the decor of the room, and even glancing at papers you might carry are simply wasted moments away from the primary target—the *eyes* of the prospect.

By maintaining eye contact you not only establish an important bridge between you and your prospect, but you do yourself a favor. You can watch to see how effective your words are, in essence, how effective your pitch is. Noting a response that may convey a negative reaction to your approach, you can gracefully shift the conversation into a slightly different channel. Noting a favorable response can give you the green light for swift advancement along a particular line of attack.

Get the Handshake Right.   Once that all-important eye contact is established, you have cleared two of the main hurdles. The third important hurdle is the handshake. But with the handshake comes the preliminary question: is the handshake expected or not? Traditionally, the handshake is expected in most business situations, especially between two people who are strangers.

However, modern rules are changing every day. With the entry of women into the work force, on an equal level with men up and down the hierarchy of management and labor, the traditional handshake sometimes is ignored.

But it is not the unisexual viewpoint that has eroded the tradition of the handshake. Actually, many executives simply do not *like* to shake hands. This can become a cliff-hanging situation for you, unless you approach it in a sensible play-it-by-ear fashion.

Beware! You may have entered the office of a person who is more insecure than you are. The prospect may simply pull back into a shell, moving behind a big desk as a kind of bunkering down behind the Maginot Line. Or the prospect may begin to fiddle with fake paperwork as you come in. Make an effort to show that you are ready to shake hands if desired, wait a moment or two for something to happen without making a move, and then shake hands if it seems appropriate. The handshake itself should be firm and brief. Be sure not to hold on too long in some kind of excess enthusiasm. Be sure also not to give the prospect a "wet fish" handshake. And, above all, be sure not to make a macho bonecrushing exhibition of strength, aggression, and iron-pumping.

Bag, Baggage, and Impedimenta. Another important problem looms during the first few seconds of communication with the sales prospect. If it is not summer, or if you have not been allowed to put your coat and briefcase somewhere as you enter the office, you are liable to be standing there with your coat over one arm and your briefcase fastened to the other. With which hand do you execute the handshake?

And, for that matter, what do you do with the coat, the hat, the scarf, or whatever?

If the prospect's assistant has not given you a place to hang your coat and if you still have it on when you enter the office, look around for a likely place to put it and ask permission to lay the coat on a chair, couch, or whatever. Do not stand around with your coat over your arm, your briefcase hanging in front of you, looking like an awkward high-school kid on a first date. Get rid of your impedimenta as gracefully as you can before proceeding. Maladroitness at this point can kill you.

You should also learn to manage your briefcase or folder so that it does not become the opposite of a good prop and instead turns into a monkey wrench in the machinery of communication. Once you have disencumbered yourself of your coat, you can then set the briefcase down unobtrusively on the floor for later retrieval.

The Right Place to Sit. Seating arrangements are very important. In a strange office, you will have only a brief moment to appraise the furnishings. If there is only one chair opposite the sales prospect's desk, you will have no trouble deciding where to sit. If there are two chairs, choose the one nearest the prospect, in a place that affords you a surface of desk to place your folder or briefcase if need be.

If both chairs are in a reasonably good spot, choose the left side if you are right-handed. It is easier to work that way. Conversely, if you are left-handed, choose the right chair. You can place your briefcase between the desk and the chair and lift up materials with your working hand.

Note: Keep an attentive eye on the condition of your carrier, whether it be a briefcase, an attaché case, or a folder. A scuffed, deteriorating briefcase can signal all kinds of negative things to a prospective client. When it sits there on your lap, looking defeated, dowdy, and seedy you look defeated, dowdy, and seedy yourself.

The Second Minute

It is pointless in this book to go into the mechanics of the sales pitch that you will be making. It is not important, at least not from the standpoint of this study of the first five minutes. What is important in this study is what you do with your eyes as you proceed with your conversation. I have already stressed that it is important to maintain good eye contact as you speak, keeping up the communication bond that you have established.

At the same time you give your attention to the prospect, however, take a look at the office environment. You can do that not only by employing peripheral vision but also by casting your eyes around as you concentrate on bringing papers out of your briefcase, or simply by breaking eye contact for a moment. It is important to do an in-depth reconnaissance of the place while seemingly focusing all attention on the prospect.

There are plenty of pieces of evidence in the office itself—clues to the personality, character, and interests of the prospect. Any one of these items may well give you a special lead through which you can help make your sale.

A Tour of the Prospect's Interests. For example, look at the photos on the walls, the books on the shelves, the trophies mounted, the products displayed, the decor of the place, the office arrangement itself. Any one of these items can give you clues as to the personal preferences of the person you are visiting. Soon enough you will pick up the habit of noting these things automatically and unconsciously the moment you enter a new environment and storing them in your subconscious for instant referral during the interview that follows.

In time you will probably pick up the knack of walking into any office, seeing everything worth noticing with a single, almost automatic glance, storing it up for future use. This is a matter of training yourself to be observant and to deduce, much in the manner of a detective on a case, character traits and personal interests from such details.

The Third Minute

Although you will have been looking at and studying the prospect from the moment you enter the office, by the third minute you should have formed some kind of opinion of the kind of person he or she is.

As I have mentioned before, however, you should never get into the habit of making snap judgments about people. Many individuals put up false fronts for a variety of reasons. Others do not try to put up masks to hide behind, but are simply not in the habit of projecting their true images.

Remember: A live human being is one of the most difficult subjects to analyze and make judgments about. What the individual does in his or her private moments may have a great deal to do with the way he or she will react in business situations. The opposite, of course, is also true.

How can you tell which kind of person your prospect is?

Well, the truth of the matter is that you cannot really tell at all. Nor can you know a person instantly. You can only know *part* of a person. But it is important that you find out as much as you can about a prospect as soon as you get into conversation.

By a little expert probing, you can usually find out a great deal within a few minutes. Once again, I stress that this is an important part of your ability to communicate rapidly and make a good impression on someone else. It takes practice and is a skill that is most handy for anyone to possess, no matter what is his or her business or personal life.

The Fourth Minute

In the first three minutes of a sales interview, it is best to keep away from the main subject at hand. The dialogue during these important minutes is generally of a gently probing nature, on both sides. Just as you want to size up the prospect and see where that individual is coming from, he or she will want to size you up to find out what kind of person you are and, if possible, where *you* are coming from.

One of the best ways to spar with one another is to open up the conversation with deliberately trivial items: the weather, the prospect's family, the business situation in general. However, there are some important dangers here. You may fall into one of the many ice-breaker traps that can be set for you.

The Trivia Trap.   The problem with using an ice-breaker to open a conversation is not that the technique is wrong—it is exactly right—but that sometimes it becomes a dead-end street. You find that you cannot proceed beyond the ice-breaker to get into the subject at hand, that is, your sale.

What sometimes happens is that you open up with a very good ice-breaker. For example, you spot a picture on the prospect's desk that shows a skiing scene. And you begin to talk about skiing; you love the sport yourself, and so on. It is an excellent ice-breaker. The prospect thaws almost immediately. A friendly conversational tone settles over the discussion.

But, quite suddenly, without any warning, the conversation falls into the hands of the prospect. He or she is moving on from skiing to water-skiing, and from water-skiing to sailboating. The prospect is expanding and cannot stop. You are unable to stop him or her either, because you are good friends by now. The prospect is into wind-surfing now, and if you broke into his or her line of thought you would be rewarded with a sneer and a sudden goodbye.

Avoid this type of trap. If the ice-breaker is appropriate, good enough. But confine yourself to it and to it alone, and when you see the conversation moving beyond that and out of your control, immediately take command as politely but as firmly as you can. Your prospect will understand. He or she may very well have avoided discussion of your product by snapping the trivia trap shut on you and will respect you for seeing the snare and for extricating yourself.

The Doom and Gloom Trap. There is another trap for you to watch out for. It is called the "business couldn't be worse" trap. By making a casual statement about business conditions, and then asking politely how the prospect's business is going, you may find yourself the recipient of a tremendously harrowing story of how bad everything in the industry is at the present time and of how miserable the prospect has been because of it.

After a few minutes of this pessimistic input, you learn that the prospect is personally standing in the breadline at the end of each day, that the family is on food stamps and supplementary subsistence, and that the spouse is taking in laundry and baking seed cakes to sell on the street corner or working three jobs to make ends meet.

Once the prospect has established such a poverty-stricken situation, your only course is to retreat out the door and out of his or her life.

To prevent this kind of outpouring of gloom and doom, make sure that you couch your questions in a specific framework. Also, make sure that your question about business tends to direct the conversation toward the product or service you are trying to sell.

The "Please Help Me" Trap. In trying to establish a friendly relationship with a prospect, you may inadvertently fall into yet another trap. This could be called the "Can you help me?" trap. What starts this type of response is a simple enough movement away from a discussion of general business to the prospect's *bad* business.

Then the prospect hints that if business were better, more materials might be bought, and so on. Implicit in this statement is the desire of the prospect to hear how his or her own business opportunities can be improved. There is a pause as the prospect waits for your sympathy and your suggestions as to what the prospect can do to make more money.

Do not fall into this trap! When you begin to suggest how prospects can improve their businesses, you are allowing yourself to fall into an obvious bottomless pit. What can you say that the prospect does not already know? After being in the business and succeeding at it so far, the prospect obviously *knows* what he or she is doing. He may be poormouthing you, but he hasn't gone bankrupt. What does he or she care about how you could help with suggestions?

Now hear this! The prospect is *not* interested in your ideas at all but is simply trying to avoid talking about your product or your service.

Make it a rule never to give gratuitous advice to prospects about businesses they know. Most of them are probably kidding you anyway, trying to make you look the fool. All of which, of course, makes them look that much better to themselves.

The Fifth Minute

By now you should be entering the point of the conversation where you usually launch into your sales pitch. Be sure to think back to the preliminary conversation to see if there have been any hints dropped about how the prospect feels about the products or services you may be representing.

Never forget that the prospect would not be seeing you without some kind of inclination to study your product. However, you have to know exactly where his or her true interests do lie before you can launch yourself into your sales presentation.

Recapitulation: It is now time to look briefly back at what has already been said during this meeting. Is there any hint as to whether or not the prospect wants the product or service you are selling? Is there any other item that *might* be preferred? Could you make a fast substitution and pitch *that*?

MOVING INTO THE PRESENTATION

Most salespersons develop an instinct for timing. There is a moment when the pitch is at optimal level. There is a moment when the prospect is ready. And that is the exact moment at which you should begin the pitch.

When does this moment occur?

Each case is different. You should be able to "feel" when the time comes. Your prospect may even make a gesture in body language or in speech that indicates the time is ripe.

Timing is harder to determine if you are engaged in a sparring match with a prospect who is trying to dodge your pitch or who has put up numerous objections and road blocks in advance. If this is the case, the best line of approach is to go on. In other words, when in doubt, pitch.

Actually, there is little to be gained by continuing to circle one another warily, looking for an opening that may never occur.

Do not let yourself be stalled in any more circumlocutions. When the time is ripe, jump in.

If you have prepared the groundwork correctly in those crucial first five minutes you will indubitably hook your fish!

9

FIVE MINUTES TO OFFICE SUCCESS

Although interviewing for a job and making a sale are activities in business that specifically involve one-on-one meetings crucial to instant communication and satisfaction, you can make use of specific meeting potentials in your routine business relationships as well, especially on an office level.

The first five minutes you spend with one of your superiors, provided you have not been interviewed by him or her already, can set the tone for your entire term of employment at a company.

The same is true of the first five minutes you spend with one of your immediate subordinates. In some ways your relationship with your subordinates may be as crucial as, or even more crucial than, your relationship with your superiors.

And the first five minutes you spend with those employees of the company who are on the same level as you are can be just as important to your happiness and satisfaction on the job.

It is time to take a look at the various ways in which you can make sure that those first five minutes are getting you off to a good start with your office colleagues and putting you on the right basis for a profitable and continued relationship.

This chapter will discuss the three important relationships between:

- You and your superiors
- You and your subordinates
- You and your peers

FIVE MINUTES TO SUCCESS
WITH YOUR SUPERIORS

In this example, I would like you to assume that the person to whom you are going to be directly responsible is a total stranger. Perhaps you have been transferred from one department to another in a company reorganization. You do not know anything at all about your new boss. You have heard rumors—who has not?—but you are smart enough not to believe hearsay *in toto*.

You want to meet this person without prejudice, without overblown fears or hopes that have nothing to do with reality, and with a clean slate on both sides of the desk.

The first order of business is to prepare yourself for the meeting as you would prepare yourself for a job interview. That is, you do everything you can to get yourself up for the meeting, enter the office with the proper physical presence, and go through the preliminaries as you would at a typical job interview.

The second order of business, once you have met and exchanged small talk, is to size up your new superior. Because there are so many different methods of sizing up people, I have decided to approach this exercise by setting up a number of categories into which a majority of people fit. Not everyone can be easily filed in a box, of course. But these four main compartments will give you an idea of what you may be getting into.

The Four Different Kinds of Bosses

There are many different types of bosses: martinets, poets, socialists, dreamers, geniuses, and so on. I think you can put most people into four general categories.

1. The conceptual boss
2. The structured boss
3. The humanitarian boss
4. The no-nonsense boss

Now let us take a look at each of these types.

1. The Conceptual Boss.   I visualize a person who is aloof, stand-offish, and impersonal as someone who might be called a "conceptual" type of individual. That is, this person is involved in abstract ideas, in concepts, in the "big picture," in imaginative undertakings. The "conceptual" person is usually expansive and somewhat dependent on intuitive responses. The conceptual person does not like to articulate facts and figures to the exclusion of all else. An idealist and a dreamer, the conceptual person pays no attention to statistical breakdowns and extrapolations. Plans and designs bore him or her. On the other hand, progress and new ideas are intriguing.

2. The Structured Boss.   I visualize the person who is businesslike, ordered, and interested in specifics as a "structured" person. This person's mind is occupied with what traditionally is looked on as "business concepts." The structured person knows what the bottom line of every sheet in the files says. The structured boss knows the salaries, the projects, the assessment sheets, the hopes and fears of each employee. The structured person knows the company's long-range and short-range plans. He or she can be detailed or expansive, can be introspective or objective, can look forward or backward in the company history, can deal with subordinates and can deal with superiors.

3. The Humanitarian Boss.   I visualize the man or woman who is really more interested in people than in typewriters, computers, or adding machines, as a true "humanitarian" person. The humanitarian is in business, of course, but is interested in the personnel and not in the product. Generally, the perfect job for the humanitarian is the personnel office, but often the humanitarian is involved with other echelons of power. This boss speaks in warm, friendly, human, and abundant terms. The humanitarian's writing style is personalized and full of warmth. Frequently, the humanitarian is involved in counseling others and in helping them through crises of a personal and professional nature.

4. The No-nonsense Boss.   I visualize the martinet type—abrupt, to the point, not hostile but not friendly either—as the "no-nonsense" type of boss. The person is one who believes fundamentally that results count more than anything else in business. The no-nonsense person has a writing style that is basic telegraphese. The tone of voice is urgent, but informal at the same time. The entire approach of the no-nonsense boss is functional. I said "martinet" at the beginning of this description, but I should refine that a bit to say "by-the-numbers" type. Although the no-nonsense boss may be singularly objective, there is always a spark of sympathy left over for the subordinate.

Classification of Your Superiors

The third order of business, after you have met and sized up your superior, is to classify that person according to these four categories. You can get a great deal of help by analyzing the person's nonverbal language: the clothes the person wears and the environment with which the person surrounds him- or herself.

For example:

The conceptual boss usually wears mixed clothing of one style or another, but is well-dressed and rather in good taste. The real tip-off to the conceptual person is the office furniture which he or she chooses. It is often futuristic, far-out in décor, a kind of art-deco redivivus.

The structured boss is the most conservative and ordinary dresser of these four types. This boss usually wears suits of an unassuming and moderate design. There is no attempt to outdo in either style or price range. The office area is usually correct and tasteful, with logically arranged desks, chairs, and bookcases.

The humanitarian boss can always be picked out of the crowd. This type of boss generally wears the most informal garb of all. Clothes tend to be colorful and tailored to the mood of the day, with the warmer colors predominating. The grooming may be informal, sometimes even tousled. The office space generally tends to the warmer colors, too, with places to sit and meditate. Such a boss likes to have windows overlooking vast areas to give the psyche a chance to wing into eternity.

The no-nonsense boss usually wears functional and utilitarian clothes of an informal nature. There is a reason for the informality; the no-nonsense boss is usually too busy to be formal in dress. That tendency spills over into office decor as well. Usually the no-nonsense boss lives in a cluttered beehive of a place, with papers sprawled everywhere, books piled in the corners, newspapers folded back to marked items. The point is obvious: This guy just is not kidding around.

How to Do unto Your Superiors

The fourth order of business after you have categorized these four types is to act accordingly; that is, to treat each as you would expect him or her to be treated.

The conceptual boss. Discuss abstractions and concepts. It is not necessary to be specific with the conceptual boss; only be imaginative and slightly vague. The big picture is the one of interest. There is no need to get down to brass tacks or hammer out anything specific in the way of *modus operandi*. Set the tone somewhere off into the twenty-first century.

The structured boss. Be businesslike, ordered, and specific in your words and ideas. Talk about organization, structure, and specifics. Comment on business trends in the general area of your own company, but then expand outward to other areas. Discuss upcoming projects he or she might have in mind.

The humanitarian boss. Discuss anything specific about personnel that you might be interested in. You can also discuss getting along with the people in the company, always fair game for the humanitarian. You can even talk about the place of government's humanitarian agencies in relation to business. Talk about your spouse, your children (if you have any), his wife, her husband, the children, and so on.

The no-nonsense boss. Be very brief and to the point. Use quick sentences, stripped of adjectives and adverbs. Speak in a staccato manner; be concise and urgent. Talk about the immediate future and the specifics of what is to be done within the next two or three days. Remember that results count with this person, nothing else.

Never—but Never!—Mix up the Categories

The purpose of your meeting with your new superior is, of course, to show that you understand exactly what kind of person he or she is, and to give the impression that you know what you are doing so he or she will not be required to check up on you all the time.

The point of analyzing your superior should be obvious: You do not want to treat your superior as the kind of person he or she is *not*. To talk to a conceptual boss as you would talk to a humanitarian boss would be a bad mistake, and vice versa.

Half the trouble in business today is the inability of many employees to understand and to comprehend their superiors, subordinates, and peers. Once that hurdle is cleared the rest is usually smooth sailing. It all depends on what you do with that first five minutes.

FIVE MINUTES TO SUCCESS
WITH YOUR SUBORDINATES

Dealing with a subordinate in the first five minutes in the office is quite different from dealing with a superior. You are in the organization to work for your superior, to do what is wanted of you, and to do what is expected. With a subordinate, you must spend the first few minutes presenting the proper image of a benevolent and understanding, though exacting, boss.

It is not at all strange to think of yourself as an authoritarian figure, no matter what kind of person you really are. But you should exude confidence, even though you do not need to lay it on with a trowel.

I was once switched over to a new manager to put out a monthly magazine for the company. He called me in to give me the lowdown about the job.

"We've got one deadline a month. I want all the copy ready for the deadline. If we miss, we'll be charged extra money by the printers. I don't care how you do the job. You can do it hanging upside down out the window if you want. But get it done by the time it's due and we'll get along fine."

We did.
I never missed a deadline, either.

How Not to Get Results

I once worked for another person in a writing capacity. About four days after I started, he called me in and said:

"If you ever turn in another piece of copy like this, I'm going to give it back to you and you know what you can wipe with it. Now get back and do it again, and this time get it right."

Needless to say, I did not work there for long. The problem was not that person's crudity of expression, but the fact that I was never apprised as to what I was supposed to be delivering in the way of copy. Since nothing was specified, I assumed that I was on my own. My own way was not his way, but no one discovered that until it was too late.

The question of the relationship of a boss to a subordinate is much more sensitive than that of a subordinate to a boss. In many ways, it is the most difficult of all relationships to establish correctly.

The Power and the Glory

Much of the problem between superior and subordinate involves the way the superior wields the power of office over the subordinates in it. Power can be used or it can be abused. If power is underused or overused, it is as good as abused, that is, under- or overused means used wrongly. Either way is as bad as the other. The main thing about the abuse of power is that it demonstrates the fact that the superior has never learned how to implement power and is uncomfortable with it.

If power is overused, the superior becomes a Simon Legree type, the kind of person who stands behind a door with a big whip just waiting for someone to make a minor mistake.

If power is underused, the superior turns into a kind of Mr. Nice Guy with a goofy grin on his puss. He lets all things slide until a serious rupture or catastrophe occurs, at which point Mr. Nice Guy is leaned on by *his* superior and then all hell breaks loose. Mr. Nice Guy becomes Mr. Hyde and heads roll.

Rights and Responsibilities

Properly exercised authority is essential in any office set-up. It begins with the establishment by the superior of an attitude of recognition of all subordinates; that is, both superior and subordinates count and both have rights and both have responsibilities.

How well you as a superior manage to establish this authority at the beginning of your regime—in that first five minutes—will determine how successful you are in your reign over those who work for you. It is best to focus on the positive aspects of the job at the very outset. And to do that, of course, you should look ahead and analyze what your duties are.

The Way to Self-appraisal

One way to clarify the job in your own mind is to give yourself a rating even before you face any of your subordinates. I suggest that you run down an ordinary job appraisal form and answer the questions about yourself. In that way you can spot, perhaps, any weaknesses or doubtful areas of the job before you find yourself being victimized by them.

Here is a typical performance-appraisal form. Take it and analyze it in relation to the job you might be undertaking as a new manager.

The form usually breaks down into four sections:

1.   Department supervision
2.   Development of personnel
3.   Leadership capabilities
4.   Business growth

1. Department Supervision.   Your main performance on a day-to-day basis will be involved in running and supervising your department. What you should look out for are organizational abilities, your follow-through on them, and your solution of strategic problems.

> **Organizational abilities.** First ask yourself how good you are at handling a workload of specific tasks. Do you set your priorities and meet your timetables with accuracy and success? Do you need development in this area? Should you warn your subordinates that they can help you here?
>
> **Follow-through.** Ask yourself if you are able to respond to problems with a sense of urgency, if you have a good record of being able to follow through on problems you have encountered before. Should you seek help here?
>
> **Strategic problems.** Ask yourself if you will be able to handle ongoing strategic problems that develop on the job. In your preliminary interview, see if you can find out if there are any strategic problems in existence in the job, and, if so, plan with your subordinates how to meet them together.

2. Development of Personnel.   You will also be trying to develop the people who work for you as you gain their cooperation and respect. What you should keep in mind is your track record in establishing yourself as a role model for your workers. Are you good at it? Are you bad at it? Do you know your potential?

Do you have a good development plan? Are you able to delegate authority so that your subordinates will all be able to function independently?

Development plan. Ask yourself if you have a good development plan in mind for the people who will be working for you. You should tell them what it is and how it functions, and where you want your department to be in six months' time.

Independent function. Ask yourself how much free rein to allow your workers. From the beginning you should let all your subordinates know exactly how much independent thinking they will be allowed and how much support they can expect from you in their separate functions.

3. Leadership Capabilities. From past experience you should know a bit about your leadership capabilities. But you will want to implant a sense of your worth in your subordinates when you first meet them. If you are a no-nonsense person, let them know that. If you are a more easygoing authority figure, let them know that. Establish your leadership role immediately so that it is clear and unblurred. Also, know about research strategies, issues and objectives, and your own presence and judgment.

Research strategies. Ask yourself how well you use the research resources of the company to help develop sound strategies of business. Do you need help here from your subordinates? Do you expect them to work in this area for you or with you?

Issues and objectives. Make sure you are good at passing on issues and objectives to your subordinates so that they will all know in what direction you intend to go. A subordinate without a clear indication of the course of action will never perform adequately. Be sure to communicate your issues and objectives to them at your very first meeting, and make sure they understand them.

Presence. Ask yourself again if your presence and personality are adequate for command of the people serving you. If you need help in establishing presence, you should try to maximize your presence before meeting with your subordinates. Your first five minutes is crucial here.

Judgment. Ask yourself how good your judgment is. A good manager must have good judgment to arbitrate differences between subordinates, or to decide between two courses of action having to do with personnel procedures. Make sure you show your subordinates, by example or by precept, how you will exercise judgment in their problems with management. You may *be* management to them, but you know that you are not management when you are dealing with *your* superiors.

4. *Business Growth.* You should impress upon your subordinates the expertise you have in the business world so that none of them gets the idea that you are a pussycat in the jungles of big business, ready to be shot down. You should manage to arouse their respect in this area immediately. Subordinates do not like to follow a leader who is flabby and self-conscious and doddering, and who does not know his or her way around in the world of business.

Building programs. Ask yourself what you know about the building programs the company has inaugurated and is carrying out. Impart to your subordinates at your first meeting the importance of the building programs that are coming up and elicit their help immediately. By working together, superior and subordinates can make this new approach work.

Program priorities. Ask yourself if you are completely aware of the company's future priorities. You must get a handle on this before you meet with your subordinates so that when you do, you can explain any priorities and long-range or immediate plans, and their implementation.

The Meaning of Meaning Business

By running through this imaginary job appraisal form and by establishing points under each category, you will be able to set up for yourself a basic program for your first meeting with subordinates. You should have it all together by the time you see any one of them. A subordinate who watches a newcomer wander tentatively through the corridors of a new office is immediately aware that the new leader does not know where it is at, and may never be able to find out. Any possible respect vanishes forthwith.

Of course, the initial self-interrogation here described is simply a means of putting together an obvious plan from which you can quote and extrapolate. The real importance of a meeting with a subordinate is to impress yourself upon him or her. You want to show the subordinate that you mean business, that you are in charge, and that you also have empathy for the problems of your subordinates and will be working together with them for the future.

The key to that first meeting is to stir up a response in those who work for you, a response that will inspire them to do the best possible for you. In turn, of course, you will do your very best for every one of your workers.

FIVE MINUTES TO SUCCESS
WITH YOUR PEERS

Decision-making meetings are probably the biggest time-wasters in the world of business. Hours and hours are spent at meetings, using up the time of many men and women. Much of that time lost needlessly and for eternity.

There are usually two reasons that there is so much wasted time.

1. Poor presentation
2. Poor listening

Getting back to the premise I stated in the first chapter of this book, the first five minutes is the most important part of any meeting in business.

- It sets the tone.
- It introduces the protagonists.
- It puts the best foot forward on both sides.

Extending this precept to the meeting room of any company, there should be a way to minimize excess verbiage, excess shillyshallying, and so on, in order to cut through the garbage and get to the point quickly.

Establishing a Clear Strategy

One of the most important things for you to do if you are involved in setting up a meeting with a group of your peers is to decide on a clear strategy at the beginning. It is a good idea to require each staff member under your control to bring to the meeting a special memorandum of no more than two pages stating the following five points:

1. The subject he or she wishes to present
2. The issue within the subject to be presented
3. Information about the subject
4. A personal recommendation (very short)
5. A conclusion

Before the meeting, send to each participant a brief agenda defining the subject or purpose of the meeting, with a review of the current status of the problem. In the agenda there is a time-lock on the meeting, a list of participants, and a time-lock on each person's discussion time.

Confine the number of participants to no more than fifteen. If a group must be larger, break it up into several sections of no more than five or six. Each unit should examine a problem and come to a decision. Then the unit sends a representative to a final meeting to make the final decision.

Be sure to sit at a position around the table where you can see all the others, especially where you can observe everyone's eyes. By a quick glance at the eyes you can be instantly aware of who is confused, who is irritated, who is approving, or who is gone for the day. At a rectangular conference table, the best place to sit is at one corner, since you can see all the people from there. You need not look at people only to get their input, but to give them feedback and instructions with your own eyes.

Start the Meeting Promptly

When you start the meeting, be sure to warn the participants of the time limit you have set. Tell them that everything must be concluded by that specific time, and stick to the schedule. Be sure to start on time. Most conferences start late, and that not only adds to the length of the meeting itself but it allows you to get off on the wrong foot by violating your first rule.

Never wait for latecomers. It is the people who have come on time who must be considered. If someone comes in later, you can always absorb him or her.

A well-planned meeting must develop momentum from the beginning. That is up to you as its chairperson. Be sure to instill a feeling of suspense and excitement the moment you begin. In that way you can wake everybody up and give them a message that you will not tolerate snores or daydreams. When you sit down in the chair, look like a leader.

Note: Most meeting-room chairs are designed to assassinate alertness and authority. They make you look casual and lounging when you sit in them. A good straight-backed chair is probably not available, but if one is, by all means grab it and use it. By forcing you to sit up straight, it gives you much more sitting-down presence—backbone, actually. It makes for an immediate exertion of energy and lively communication and you absolutely cannot doze off in a hard-backed chair.

When you talk, be sure you look in turn into the eyes of each person seated at the table leaving out no one. Do not click or twirl your pen, twist and untwist paper clips, pick your nails, or anything else. Be sure to be animated when you speak. Even when the subject is a serious one, it is not a funeral. Live it up.

Monitoring for Feedback

Make sure you check for feedback from everyone at the table. You can gauge exactly how well or how badly you are doing by monitoring every eye at the table. By all means check body language too. If your listeners are doodling or looking apathetic or seem to be dreaming, perhaps about skiing or swimming, pick up the pace of your statements.

Once the meeting gets under way, make sure the pace continues at an animated clip. If it should slow down, act like a circus ringmaster, crack the whip and move the meeting along with energy and dispatch.

Take notes as others speak. Watch out for the dawdling speaker who will tend to slow down the pace that you want to keep alive. If you feel you should cut down the long-winded speaker, do not hesitate to do so.

Here's how to do it.

1. Study the long-winded speaker's timing.
2. Observe the breathing rhythm as he or she talks.
3. Pick up the spots where he or she takes a breath.
4. At the hesitation, break in with a statement.
5. Immediately turn to another participant and encourage him or her to contribute.

The long-winded speaker will never be quite sure what happened, but you will have put the dawdler *hors de combat*.

And good riddance!

Make Evaluations on Everybody's Input

Exert discipline in your own listening habits. Be sure to respect the opinions of others and comment on these opinions in any productive way possible. As you chair the meeting, be sure to evaluate everyone's contributions fairly and encouragingly.

Listen to any disagreements. Encourage discussion. Do not allow any one protagonist to take over to the exclusion of the others. Even though every group has certain people in it who tend to lead, do not let anyone get out too far in front of the rest.

Remember that you are the chairperson. It is up to you to let everyone air his or her opinion.

In general:

• Be fair.
• Be considerate.
• But be *in control*.

Checklist for Committee Chairpersons

Keep a list of these tips in your notebook for reference. They will help you keep things going if you come to an impasse of any kind.

- ✔ Begin with a tight agenda that covers all the subjects involved.
- ✔ Stick to the point. Make sure no one strays from the subject.
- ✔ Do not be too polite with your peers. Make sure that you are not a pushover.
- ✔ When someone raises an irrelevant point, do not let it pass. Immediately pick it up by saying, "Let's hold that for discussion later. Now we're covering something else."
- ✔ Encourage everyone to answer the question asked, even if you have to repeat it.
- ✔ Do not allow anyone to twist the question into a platform for a completely irrelevant statement.
- ✔ Always begin a meeting by summing up what was said and decided on at the previous meeting (at least if there *was* a previous meeting).
- ✔ Try to think of some way to motivate your participants to discuss the questions and the answers.
- ✔ Treat the entire meeting as if it were all the *first five minutes*.
- ✔ Remember that peers are as difficult to handle correctly as a superior or a subordinate.
- ✔ Make the committee what it is *supposed* to be, a meeting of the minds—of *superior* minds, at that.

10

THE IMPORTANCE OF FEELING IMPORTANT

By now you should know the importance of that first five minutes when you are trying to establish a one-on-one business relationship with another person.

By now you should have learned something new about putting your best foot forward in such an important situation.

By now you should know how to use that first five minutes in building toward successful meetings and contacts in the business world.

You are, in fact, almost ready to go out and make use of those three hundred seconds to turn the business world into a better place for you.

Well, almost.

Actually, not quite yet.

We are not yet through all the lessons.

THERE IS SOMETHING MISSING

So far, I have been concentrating on showing you the importance of the first impression that you make on someone else. I have been concentrating on preparing you to put your best foot forward during those crucial moments. I have been telling you how to speak, how to listen, how to use nonverbal communication, how to dress, how to mold yourself the proper persona, how to work a job interview, how to make a sale, and how to be successful in the business world in general.

That is, I have been concentrating on *you*.

You will note, if you think about it for a moment, that there is one element missing.

In any communication situation—a conversation is the most obvious example—there are always *two* people involved.

What about the *other* person?

Indirectly, I have mentioned that "other" person, calling him or her "your communicant," or whatever.

So far I have stressed what *you* should do to impress the other person.

So far I have never really touched upon that other person at all, except as an object to focus upon or an object to be manipulated.

The Story of Ella of the Cinders

I would like to bring that other person to life and let you see what makes him or her tick. I would like to show you how you can touch that other person with a magic wand and transform the dull charwoman Ella of the Cinders into Cinderella, the Epitome of Beauty.

How?

A good question.

How, indeed.

For the moment I intend to abandon the more direct path that I have been taking and circle around just a bit.

Awakening the Sleeping Princess.   What does the subtitle, "Awakening the Sleeping Princess" mean, anyway?

Are *you* the sleeping princess I am talking about?

In no way.

The sleeping princess is that *other* person who you must, by a touch of the magic wand, bring to stunning life.

The sleeping princess in the subtitle is "your communicant"—in other words, the person with whom you are trying to establish a bond of communication.

How come?

I am going to be devious and illustrate this point by a couple of allegorical references that may look like diversions at first but actually are not.

From Soot to Stardom.   The craftsmanship, subtlety, and outright artistry of the composers of epics and romances, of sagas and fairy tales, have always amazed me.

Consider the fairy tale, that is, the epitome of *all* fairy tales—the one called *Cinderella.*

In *Cinderella* you have a nice young woman who, through fate, has lost her mother and has been saddled with a stepmother and three ugly, evil stepsisters. She is relegated to sweeping out the cinders in the fireplace, the lowest position in the hierarchy of society.

But, on the evening of the grand ball celebrated by the country's handsome young unmarried prince, when the sisters and the step-mother are all togged out in their most garish and tasteless fashion, Ella of the Cinders has to sit on the hearth by the chimney, keeping the soot company. She is not allowed to *see* the prince, much less *meet* him.

Once the uglies have left the house, suddenly a fairy god-mother appears, touches Ella with a magic wand, and lo! she is transformed into a beautiful woman, dressed in her contemporary finest, complete with a bejeweled coach to transport her to the palace.

At that moment, Ella of the Cinders becomes *someone.* Until that magic second, she has been *no one.* Now she is an entity, now she is important.

And *how* important! At the ball, she catches the prince's eye, she dances with him until midnight, but then sinks once again to her lowly state. Until . . . of course, you know the rest.

The Metamorphosis of Ella.   But for a moment analyze the point of the storyteller who is spinning this yarn. The point of the tale, the crux of its magic, is the moment at which Ella of the Cinders changes to Cinderella the Epitome of Beauty.

How does this plain, untutored woman suddenly achieve true beauty?

Through the wave of a magic wand, you may say.

I say no.

I say that she becomes beautiful, as many women—and men as well—become beautiful (or handsome) because she is suddenly and unexpectedly made to feel *important!*

It is the fairy godmother who makes her feel important, who brings Ella to life by telling her that she *is* believed in, that she *is* beautiful, that she *is* a person of repute and honor. The wand is the storyteller's symbol of psychological metamorphosis, of efflorescence.

And so, because Ella *believes* she is beautiful and important, she shines at the ball. Not for one moment should anyone believe that all her clothes are real, that the coach is really made of jewels. The point is, she becomes radiant and lovely because she has been *touched by someone else.*

That is what the story *really* says.

While she is sitting in the cinders, a voice from somewhere out there speaks to Ella:

"You are better than your sisters. You are prettier than they are, *if you try*. Now go to that ball, and shine, Cinderella!"

And Cinderella does just that.

All right, Cinderella is only one fairy story. All the rest are about hobgoblins, dwarfs, and beanstalks that go berserk on plant food.

Right?

Wrong again.

The Transformed Princess

Take the next most popular fairy story, the tale of *Snow White and the Seven Dwarfs*. Again, the crux of this story is the transformation of a Plain Little Girl into a Beautiful Princess. No matter the fact that the Wicked Witch feeds her poisoned apples—shades of the serpent in the Garden of Eden! The point of the tale is that the Plain Little Girl eventually lies encased in total catalepsy as if in a block of ice, lies for years simply waiting to be brought back to life by a kiss delivered by a handsome prince.

Again, it is through the magic of someone else's intervention that she is returned to life. What happens? Through a series of convoluted plot machinations that vary from one version of the story to the next, a handsome prince is led to her and kisses her as she lies there seemingly dead, immediately transforming her into a beautiful, vibrant princess.

Now, you simply cannot believe that Snow White was really dead and has been brought back to life by a man's kiss, do you? Of course not. She was only *symbolically* dead, encased in a block of ice that symbolizes shyness, unable to project her emotions and her desires to anyone else. Once the prince touches her and transforms her, she comes to life and . . . again, you know the rest.

As I see it, here again the magic of resurrection is simply used to disguise a rather mundane fact of life.

Waiting for the Chance to Shine

Everyone, these stories tell me, is waiting around for a chance to be alive, to be vital, to shine in the presence of friends and acquaintances. Everyone is temporarily in suspended animation, much as was Snow White. Everyone is working in the chimney sweeping out the ashes, like Ella of the Cinders, waiting to be transformed.

The sleeping princess is out there waiting to be brought back to life. It is obvious what you must do about it.

You must bring that comatose individual alive by touching him or her with the magic wand of your own interest, your own attention, your own excitement.

It is *you* who must claim responsibility for awakening the sleeping princess. Do not for the moment think that I am limiting the gender to the female by calling the character in the story "princess." The princess can be a prince just as easily as not. There are men who lie dormant waiting to be brought to life, just as there are women waiting to be touched and revitalized by the right person.

The Magic of Resurrection

Sure, fairy tales are for kids. But they contain trade secrets that can illuminate the lives of all of us. And I believe that those two fairy tales really contain the crux of something I feel to be most important in business today, the need to animate and bring to life businesspersons who do not know how to animate themselves.

That includes most everyone out there.

For the moment, I want to look at a more modern myth, the myth of the businessman who never made it. How many of you can say with certainty that you *did* make it? Oh, very well, but now you can sit down. It is the rest of you I want to address.

THE MYTHOS OF MODERN SUCCESS

In *Death of a Salesman* Arthur Miller has modernized the myth of success by turning it upside down and writing about a sheep dressed in wolf's clothing, rather than a wolf dressed in sheep's clothing. Willie Loman is a loser who is playing a self-assigned role of winner.

At the climax of Act III of the drama, when Willie realizes what he is and sinks down into a catatonic impassivity, reacting with revulsion at the truth about himself, his wife addresses the heavens and cries out what I think of as the key statement of the play:

Attention, attention must be finally paid to such a person.

The speech is perhaps a convoluted and inside-out aphorism, but it certainly has a ring of truth in today's world where an entertainment celebrity is assassinated in the streets of New York in order to satisfy the inner longings of his murderer to have his name associated with that celebrity, even in death!

- A dog barks frantically for no apparent reason.
- A child screams raucously in a crib.
- An unknown individual screams furiously in the night.

An uninterested observer notes those typical actions and shrugs his shoulders, hitting the nail of truth on the head and says:

"He just wants attention."

The Meaning of Attention

Actors, actresses, politicians, professionals of all kinds in every line of business endeavor—all such people pay money to have their names appear in newspaper columns or in magazine articles. They are paying for what the rest of us do not have the money or the actual need to finance: public recognition.

Free translation: Attention!

It is a mistaken concept, but it is a very much believed one, that you do not live until you are recognized, are paid attention to, are talked about.

- Everyone wants to be noticed.
- Everyone wants attention paid to him or her.
- Everyone wants to *feel* important.

That is the key to awakening the sleeping princess or prince, and *that* is the real reason for getting yourself together and taking your act on the road in the business world. *That* is the real way to make someone else say to you, after only five minutes of conversation:

"I like you. I really like you. And I want to do business with you."

The True Prince or Fairy Godmother

My point in leaving this most important concept to the end of the book is an obvious one. You can see what it is if you think it through. Making a business contact feel important by focusing attention on him or her, and the *way* you make that business contact feel important, is dependent totally on your own *presence,* on your style, your own persona, as we have discussed it through the pages of this book.

It is absolutely necessary for you to be totally at your best when you play the fairy godmother or the handsome prince in business. It is only someone who is together and "up" for a meeting who can, in five minutes, transform a dormant nonentity into a lively, alert, awakened, and glowing sleeping beauty who will help pull off the business deal of the century.

Because this added concept may put a whole new aspect on first impressions, I am going to recapitulate my most important points, and show you how they fit in with this new facet of making others feel important in order to get them to feel good about you, to like you in return, and to *want* to do business with you.

FIFTEEN FACETS OF BUSINESS CHARACTER

I told you already to try to concentrate on several facets of character in order to hone yourself into the most authoritative, most convincing, and most credible person possible. I want to take those concepts and think about them once again.

1. Authority
2. Certainty
3. Consideration
4. Credibility
5. Empathy
6. Inspiration
7. Integrity
8. Intimacy
9. Luster
10. Presence
11. Resolution
12. Self-assurance
13. Understanding
14. Vigor
15. Vivacity

I told you I wanted you to consider these facets at all times, until you found yourself acting them out in a visible way. Now you can see what I was getting at. In order to impress someone else enough to awaken that someone from the catalepsy of being unnoticed and ignored, you must exude the proper *presence* to be believed.

The Decline and Fall of the Anti-hero

If you go into a business situation in which you want to make someone else *feel* important and you are playing a Woody Allen anti-hero role with a loser complex, you are most definitely *not* going to awaken the other person to anything but a nightmare of ineffectualness.

What I am saying is that a fairy godmother or a handsome prince must always go into a situation of resurrection with the proper mind-set and the proper outside *look* and *presence* of a magician who can do the trick.

And so, to get your house in order for this feat, you must prepare yourself to *look* the part.

FINDING THE PROPER VOICE

Because the way you say things and the way you use your voice are so important in the creation of an image of strength and authority, I gave you a number of tips on how to use your voice in the proper manner to establish a businesslike rapport with someone else.

Now that you can see what you are trying to do in your first five minutes with another person, you can understand why your voice has to be properly trained and attuned to the right communication level.

It was the fairy godmother's *voice* that impressed Ella of the Cinders, as well as her well-groomed appearance. When she told Ella that the pumpkin was a coach, Ella *believed* it. When she told Ella that Ella had glass slippers on, the girl *believed* it. That was the convincer. The godmother knew how to *say it right*.

You must always keep these points in mind when you are trying to make a business associate believe in his or her importance. The most vital thing to watch out for is the inadvertent slip of the tongue that turns the whole performance shoddy and lends it an air of falsity and phoniness. These are concepts that you do not want to have slip out, ever.

Getting the Voice Right

Take care to avoid the pitfalls of speaking in an unbusinesslike manner by making sure you follow these general rules:

- Stop, look, listen, and *then* speak!
- Consistency is the key to speaking well.
- Speak softly and be heard further.
- Always speak the truth about yourself.
- Speak formally and avoid contempt.
- Listening is the first step in speaking.
- Do *not* try to be amusing—it *ain't* funny!
- Avoid obscenity like the plague.
- Avoid euphemisms like the plague.
- Avoid slang, jargon, and gobbledegook.

THE ART OF CREATIVE LISTENING

I also spent some time on a discussion of the importance of listening rather than talking, simply because so many people who are trying to get others to pay attention to them keep talking and do *not* listen. If you *do* listen to someone who is trying to be somebody, you will already awaken in him or her an excitement in the knowledge that you are indeed listening.

I also discussed creative listening, or active listening, and the tricks of involving yourself in the conversation through comments, body language, and other ways, to keep the continuity of the conversation going on in the proper direction and at the proper speed.

The main point in listening is to remind you, and everyone else, that conversation and communication are a two-way street. They are not—repeat, *not*—just *talking*.

SPEAKING WITH THE BODY

Nonverbal language, known as body language, is a distinct adjunct of conversation, and as I said, it conveys emotions and impressions four times as strongly as verbal language. Nonverbal language comes in very handy in imparting your interest to a person and should be most important in trying to make someone else believe he or she is being listened to, paid attention to, and buoyed by intensive awareness.

You can make someone else feel important by confining your body language to an awareness of that person's presence. However, you must think it out beforehand. If you are a six-footer, you do not want to tower over someone else who is only five feet eight; that is no way to make the shorter person *feel* important. In fact, it creates exactly the opposite impression.

If the other person is very tall or very short, you should try to consider the best way to minimize the awkward difference of your sizes. It is necessary to give someone else the impression of strength and of being on the same wave length even if there is a great disparity in sizes.

During the first five minutes of a conversation, you should keep a constant lookout for the body language displayed by the other person to see if your objective of instilling confidence and belief in him or her is working out or not.

CLOTHES MAKE THE PERSON

My point in trying to give you the proper tips on grooming in the business world was to make your appearance not too overbearing, but sharp and distinctive at the same time. Good grooming is not an exercise to turn you into a peacock or a peahen, but to get you to dress in accordance with your own predetermined character, to make yourself appear to be exactly what you want yourself to be.

In other words, your clothes should enforce the image you have been at pains to project already, the image that shows you to be self-confident, empathic, responsive, and charismatic.

By dressing the part, you arouse a feeling of confidence in any business person with whom you are in contact. By being able to inspire confidence, you can then in turn help make that person feel important and good about himself or herself.

The wrong clothes and the wrong kind of grooming can throw everything out of focus and can cause you to lose control over others. In turn, this will destroy your ability to create self-confidence and optimism in others, because you do not have it yourself.

Remember! Honesty in clothing is every bit as important as honesty in self. The reason for that is a simple one: It's not nice to fool Mother Nature!

GETTING YOUR ACT TOGETHER

In giving you ways to try to get yourself together, that is, getting yourself in synchronization with yourself, I was trying to point out the easiest and surest way to find out who you are and what you are. Only by being all together and by being your real self can you project the proper image. And only by being together can you hope to make other people feel important in being touched by you.

I tried to make a case for "style" and to show you how to put yourself into a better form if you are dissatisfied with your present appearance. But I did warn you that the new you should be the real you, every bit as much as the present you is you.

Most important, I warned you to get to know yourself—to find out exactly what you are and what you want out of life. I warned you to get to know also what you are not, to make sure you are not trying to be something you do not want to be or cannot ever hope to be.

And I tried to show you how to overcome self-consciousness, the worst of all stumbling blocks to success in business.

INCREASING YOUR SELF-CONFIDENCE

I even gave you a list of ways to increase your self-confidence.

Be thoroughly aware of your strengths and your weaknesses before you set any goals for yourself.

———

Do not limit yourself by memories of past happenings that have a negative impact on you.

———

In building a persona for yourself, choose the things that you value the most in life in order to make yourself honestly *you*.

———

No one is completely unattached from the past, from the present, or from the future.

———

Do not blame yourself for every setback that occurs in your life. Many reversals are caused by things that you cannot control.

———

Try to avoid any feeling of guilt or shame over your own actions. Shame is a personal and individual assessment unrelated to deeds. Guilt is excess baggage that never helps make the trip in life an easy one.

———

Be tolerant of others and allow them to make mistakes without being hypercritical. Be tolerant of your own mistakes as well.

———

Always be open to evaluation by others, as well as by yourself. What you do should be open to improvement at all times.

———

Avoid falling into the habit of putting yourself down. A self-pitying attitude does not get people to like you any more. In fact, many resent a whiner.

———

Do not allow a person, a job, or a situation to become a stumbling block to your progress. Pass by it as soon as you can.

———

Take time out to relax, to meditate, to enjoy hobbies and recreational hours. Allow yourself quality time to get in tune with yourself.

———

Examine carefully each failure and disappointment in your life. From these analyses you can learn how to do things right and avoid such mistakes in the future.

———

Be sure to let others know what you want from them. Also let other people know what you can do *for* them.

———

Keep evaluating your progress all the time as you go along. Then you can make changes as you learn by trial and error.

———

If you experience a very deep hurt, do not let it disturb your progress. Ego is a strong thing. Turn the other cheek and forge on ahead.

———

It is a must to be completely in charge of your direction in life at all times. If things do not come out the way you want them to, try again or redirect your activities somewhere else.

And, of course, if you are indeed in charge of your life, you will have the confidence and the ability to help others mold their own lives into better channels as well.

THE MAGIC OF CHARISMA

Charisma is a bit on the magical side and might be thought by some to have no place in the business world, but I disagree. This emotional wave of excitement comes from an inner core of true enthusiasm. For most people, letting emotion show on the surface is a difficult thing. Even in a business situation, it is good to loosen up a bit in order to let your inner feelings shine through to others. It makes you look less like a cold-hearted manipulator.

I advised you to be natural, be uninhibited, be yourself, and let the real you attract others. That is the way you can make others feel better and help them learn to cope more easily with their own lives—all because of your charisma.

I told you that by letting everything inside come outside, by being completely honest about yourself and letting your innermost feelings show, you would project a charismatic image in all your business dealings.

Of course, it is obvious now that if you do affect others positively with your own charisma, you will have a lot better chance of making them feel better about themselves and about their charisma as well.

You may be able to help someone else to gain a bit of charisma by showing off your own. Charisma does arise from feelings of enthusiasm and excitement, and is similar to the feeling of being important, of being noticed, of being *somebody*. If you can impart that to someone else in those crucial first five minutes, you will have made that person feel important, and because of that feeling the person will be attracted to you.

Charisma is magical in that it can be shared with others.

THE IMPORTANT PARAMETERS OF INTIMACY

I discussed the various aspects of intimacy, pointing out how someone may come on too strong with another person and wreck a perfectly valid chance for a business relationship that could be successful. I even went into a lot of technical measurements dreamed up by psychologists in order to break down the various phases of intimacy, my Four Seasons of Intimacy, which are:

1. The eye season
2. The body season
3. The lean season
4. The touch season

Remember: Do not use all the four seasons of intimacy at the same time, unless you happen to be in a particularly intimate and long-lasting relationship. Definitely do not even approach the third or fourth seasons in an ordinary business relationship. For the first five minutes—which is what this book is about!—confine yourself strictly to the first two, and do not depend too heavily on the second. And that is *all!*

GOING ON THE ROAD

I included three chapters discussing the details of three very important different but specific situations in which you can make use of the first five minutes in establishing a good relationship with someone else in the business world.

1. At the job interview
2. On a sales call
3. On the office level

AWAKENING THE SLEEPING PRINCESS

If you look back you can see that all the rules and tips I gave you were developed to help you over those first five minutes of a business meeting with anyone else: a person of the same sex or a person of the opposite sex.

And you can see now why I was so involved with persuading you to get yourself together so that the impression you make is the proper one. You need to speak in the right way, to look right, to be yourself, to use the tricks of charisma, and to know how to proceed correctly in order to make that final contact with the person you are trying to impress with your businesslike manner.

If you are still with me, you can certainly see the need to awaken the sleeping princess in the person you are trying to influence in a business way. Almost everyone at one time or another is a cube of ice, under a spell, or simply cursed asleep into immobility. Almost everyone at some time is unable to move, to be natural, to do the right thing in life, to live it up to the hilt.

How to Be a Magic Wand

You can easily be the magic wand that wakes up someone else. By touching him or her with that wand of attention, you can create a feeling of importance and individuality in him or her, which, in turn, will make that person feel your own attraction and your own honest interest.

Is there any better way to use that first five minutes than in creating a living bond of communication, a two-way avenue of emotional and personal connection, that will serve as a bridge to a true business relationship between the two of you?

Is there any better way to spend three hundred seconds than in getting Cinderella on the way to the ball or Snow White on the way to being kissed by Prince Charming?

I cannot think of any, myself.

Try it and see.

INDEX

ABOUT THE AUTHOR

NORMAN KING credits the principles in this book with making him a multimillionaire. As one of the foremost media and marketing consultants in the country, his expertise is sought by major agencies and advertisers worldwide.

King changed the world of advertising by creating the first media buying service. He is chairman of the board of American Marketing Complex, Inc., International Association of Travel Clubs Ltd., Male Potency Centers of America, Inc., and Tele-Movies International.

He is the acknowledged dean of barter advertising and was named by *Advertising Age* as one of the ten people who made advertising news in America for three consecutive years.

King lectures widely and has authored seven books, including *The Money Messiahs,* a Book-of-the-Month—Fortune Book Club selection.

Educated at Cornell, New York University, and New York University Law School, Norman King lives with his family in New York City.